Moneyfree

An Idea Whose Time Has Come

Alan Halverson

Moneyfree
Copyright© April 2016
by Alan R. Halverson

Library of Congress
Cataloging in Publication Data

**ISBN-13:
978-1530640690**

**ISBN-10:
1530640695**

*1st Edition
April 2016*

Published by
CreateSpace

Printed in the United States of America

CONTENTS

Dedication

This presentation is dedicated to all

the eternal souls in this universe

who have a mission to share

their awareness of truth

light and love with

all others ready

to receive

them

~

Introduction

Money manipulation and money accountability have been the twin scourges of human endeavor since the dawn of civilization and have together prevented the human dream of true value living from ever becoming a reality.

That truth suggests that there must be a better way to live that dream, and this presentation provides a step by step approach to making that dream a reality.

Moneyfree does not necessarily mean living in a world without money and having no means of establishing fair exchange for goods and services rendered.

What makes better sense is to say it is freedom from slavery that money and burdensome money accountability has forced upon most of the citizens of a global economy that is now overdue for a grand transformation.

The means for a makeover that allows adequate access to money when needed seem to be always out of reach for many in the world community who need it the most.

Ever since the creation of currency, far too much of it has fallen into the hands of the controllers who have little inclination to help society solve the real issues of life.

This seemingly unavoidable gridlock can rightfully be called *moneyclot* (the lack of proper money flow to where it can nourish the economy to do the most good and benefit all to a reasonable degree).

Associated with moneyclot is the insidious side-effect called *strict monetary accountability* that results in the leading cause of an inefficient economy driven by the manipulators that consistently find ways to tie the hands of entrepreneurs who want to help us experience a better way of living.

Introduction

Many entrepreneurs would like to develop the means for an improved standard of living not only in terms of goods and services, but in peace of mind with living in a healthy environment free of significant threat due to the ravages of manmade pollution and limitation of resources.

Those who call themselves progressives understand that any budget characterized by so-called 'out-of-control-spending' is not the real issue of a troubled economy.

Unfortunately this issue is often pointed out by many others who insist on promoting the strange belief that the 'national debt' is out-of-control and must be curtailed.

Many progressives also understand that an imbalance such as a recession, a depression or a period of inflation is not the true cause of economic malaise in a system strictly driven by the accountability of money.

It is clear to many logical thinkers that these issues are only symptoms of a real disease based upon out-of-control accumulation of easy personal gain through manipulation of investments, unethical management and the quest for more money from any source to control others with it.

They correctly understand that the system itself is the out-of-control problem created by the misuse of money.

Consider for example how this has affected our world society over the space of many generations.

Since money is supposed to be the means to regulate fair exchange for goods and services, a healthy economy must rely on a smooth flow of adequate money just as any living organism must rely on an unrestricted flow of blood supply to deliver the vital nutrients and energy needed by all the supporting cells.

Clearly analogous to a restricted flow of blood, when money stops flowing smoothly and efficiently throughout the entire economy, it gets accumulated and misused by people in power to control others by withholding funding for healthy job growth and resource distribution.

10

Introduction

The result is often a desperate scramble by those with inadequate income to seek additional subsistence from any source they can find to try to garner enough income to pay for even the bare essentials.

In their scramble, their health often suffers and creates additional stress on their budget to pay the costs of health and medical care trying to remain healthy enough to work long hours to keep up their wheel-spinning pace of living.

Though it was hardly recognized as such over the ages, it was always moneyclot in one form or another that was the primary cause of most of the outward symptoms of a troubled society, including economic stagnation, lack of medical treatment, crime, poverty and the infamous gulf between the 'haves' and the 'have-nots'.

Progressives understand that the underlying need for a healthy economy is to have all people within that system have access to whatever life has to offer; otherwise no one can move forward to a sustained level of true abundance.

When that doesn't happen, complex forces come into play that subtly undermines the quality of life for everyone including those who prevent a smooth flow of money.

For example, consider the CEOs, investment czars, rock stars, high-profile attorneys, and others of the so-called wealthy elite status that acquire much of their wealth without contributing significant value to the economy to benefit the common good.

As long as someone is either famous or just a person of notoriety, all he or she has to do is write something or get a willing writer to do it, call it a book and then get a publisher to promote it as a 'best seller' whether or not it contains anything of real value.

The result is that since this person is already well-known, he or she can accumulate royalties to expand one's already unearned financial base of monetary accrual.

Many get wealthy by satisfying the needs of others to reinforce a false sense of superiority by depicting the dark side of reality for comparison against their own sense of inflated self-worth.

By constantly depicting a world filled with senseless violence, political conflict, sexual frustration, and relentless pursuit of wealth, many get the false assurance of being better than most, and therefore conclude that they deserve all the wealth they can accumulate.

By adversely affecting flow of money in an otherwise healthy economy, the stagnation of moneyclot has stymied much of humanity's social progress and aggravated other problems including fears about 'terrorism', war, poverty and disease, destruction of highways and bridges, shortage of resources, and difficulty in coping with natural disasters.

Upper, middle, lower and poverty class polarizations have forced most incomes up or down with little or no regard to a person's true worth and value as a contributor.

The lower and middle classes experience an increasing erosion of purchasing power while many end up spinning their wheels trying to reverse the trend without success.

As a result, much of the world's wealth ends up short-circuited and diverted into the hands of the affluent who keep the process going from one generation to the next as long as there are no legal means to prevent it.

The system lets a healthy flow of money turn into the moneyclot hoard accumulated by the wealthy that control vast sums effectively taken out of the economy.

Typical of the wealthy elite are the heads of businesses, corporations, sports and entertainment stars, the politically affluent and corrupt dictatorships of foreign nations.

Meanwhile, many entrepreneurs who need that money for worthwhile purposes rarely get it because the affluent continue to acquire much more than they need or deserve.

No matter what ethnic background we originate from, many of us having even a cursory vision for the future see the need for a new paradigm that finally disallows the use of money for anything other than the acquisition of goods and services necessary for a reasonable quality of life.

In fact, many of us see that one root cause of many of society's ills and limitations is the way money is viewed, used and valued as the 'end all' of a happy existence.

And the fear of going below zero in one's personal bank account is so instilled and mercilessly beaten into our consciousness that the simple values of life so cherished many ages ago are often shoved into the background of awareness about our true purpose on this planet.

As a result, the focus of trying to maintain a fair and equitable system that works for everyone has largely been abandoned amidst the flurry of maintaining legalities over the use of money and strict money accountability.

These legal limitations tend to burden everyone, yet hit the middle class, the lower class and the destitute the very hardest, because their livelihoods are now centered around the need to constantly scrape for enough income to pay their bills, and in many cases get food just to stay alive.

This presentation suggests an alternative to money and money accountability to bring into focus a totally different kind of economy without moneyclot, bills, taxes or debt.

These ideas are not new, but the end game may seem a bit more plausible if we read and consider the steps we can take right now to help make the implementation of a true moneyfree economy a dynamic reality.

~1~
The Concept

The question you might be asking is: How can we live in a world without money?

The answer: If money is meant simply as a response to 'value received for value earned'...we can't.

If we define a new word called 'moneyfree', we could!

The rest of the story offers some logical reasons as to how a step-wise set of changes in our thinking can lead to a better realization of how a new and holistic definition of moneyfree would work and operate successfully.

Relative to how money is defined and forced upon all of us right now, it is true that we have to pay for all goods and services that life offers.

It is true that society requires payment for all those things in terms of money accountability, so in that sense, there is no such thing as a free lunch.

But the bigger question one needs to ask and get an answer for is: 'How free does 'moneyfree' really mean?'

It all depends on how we look at it, or maybe to what level of relative truth we are thinking about when we ask the question, since the term is relative to a specific context and the specific extent of use intended.

Before we give an answer to the question, let's picture what a moneyfree world might look like if money (as we know it now) was officially removed from the economy and not allowed to be reproduced or used anywhere.

Just for a moment, try to imagine a classless society where every person on earth contributes for the mutual benefit and the common good of everyone else through mutual trust and cooperation.

1 The Concept

Imagine moneyfree to actually mean maximized free enterprise resulting in no bills to pay, no accumulation of debt, no necessity to borrow, no checks to write, no coins or paper money and no gold stashed away in a safe.

Visualize a global society as having nothing to do with what we now call money and all the accountability we are now constrained to do business with.

Visualize a free exchange of goods and services leading to abundance of every necessary product and service for subsistence plus a reasonable quality of life on top of all that to be made available for every man, woman and child on the face of the planet!

That may be the ultimate definition of moneyfree, but there's so much more that should be said in terms of how that plan of operation could actually be achieved.

And that is what the rest of this book will attempt to do in a logical and straightforward manner.

Right now when we go to get something of necessity that belongs to someone else, then short of beg, borrow or steal, we have to be 'accountable' and pay for it with some form of currency called money.

Or we have the option to buy it on credit and create some type of debt, so there's apparently no way around the fact that we must use money of one form or another to get virtually everything we need to survive and live comfortably with on this planet.

Short of advising anyone to rob, steal, extort or beg for a living, how about an alternative where no one has to be dishonest, and no one has to borrow, and no one has to even present money for the goods and services that life has to offer, and everyone is happy about it?

A related question – What would it take to convince every human on the face of the planet that money is no longer necessary to do business, to prosper, to be happy at their job doing the things they love to do while living a healthy life style in a pollution free environment?

1 The Concept

Many are beginning to wonder whether a strict policy of requiring money given in exchange for value received is still necessary in an age where technology and industrial innovation can now produce and deliver all the basics to every man, woman and child without requiring hard labor, long hours and stressful competition from anyone.

Without answering these questions right away, let's take a look at a significant problem out of many examples regarding what has happened since the system of money and money accountability was strictly imposed upon all of us since time immemorial…

Most of us still have or have had gainful employment throughout our working years for the primary purpose of making a living and paying the bills.

When our employer doesn't pay us enough for us to provide for reasonable living expenses easily, we find that we are under stress and continuous worry to find a way to cope and meet our obligations of money accountability.

If the gap between our reasonable expenses and our inadequate income grows wider, (as it often does), our stress and worry begin to affect all aspects of our physical, mental and emotional health, and in extreme cases may cause a complete breakdown of our ability to cope.

If we find ourselves in this situation, then at best we set up defenses to try to maintain a budget that covers all necessary expenses and still allows enough discretionary spending to make us believe we have a comfortable life.

But the problem for middle and lower class income families is that what started out as a comfortable living style often ends us slipping away due to imbalances in the economy such as inaccessible resources, increased prices, higher taxes, inflation or recession, etc.

In spite of intelligent planning, many families find that their financial health may eventually deteriorate into severe poverty or critical illness without adequate medical care.

1 The Concept

It may even become a desperate attempt to survive on one's own devises until death ultimately (and sometimes tragically) ends the struggle.

No matter what day and age we have lived in over countless generations past, most of us have known very well how our quality of life can go downhill as a result of concerns over money and money accountability that often takes control of our lives to our detriment.

So what else is wrong with this picture?

Quite a bit I would say!

It appears that the underlying cause of situations like this along with related issues involving quality of life can be traced to the derailment of focus on life's true values.

Indeed it comes down to money manipulation and the accountability of monetary balance in every bank account in existence that has forced us all into a system that places more value on business profit for personal gain rather than on providing abundance for the good of all.

Humankind's priorities of basic self-interest, religious ideologies, mistrust, intolerance, arrogance and obsession to compete for everything have played major roles in the breakdown of a potentially great society that may have once had a semblance of joyful living to allow more time for individual creativity to blossom for everyone.

Monetary concerns now take up so much of our time and energy that there is very little left for the pursuit of our natural abilities in the field of the arts, the sciences, the world of music, the theater and the world of ecology, etc.

It has become difficult to maintain a balance between civilization's advance and an infinite reservoir of spiritual values where our true purpose lies.

Through traditional ignorance of life's true purpose, it has become the rule that the prime motivator and driving force of acceptable definitions of success involves a game called competition instead of a trust called cooperation.

1 The Concept

We have ignored the basic hierarchy of human need in favor of mindless personal priority pursuits, intolerance of alternatives, lack of adequate funding for education and clean energy, and disrespect for the rights, opinions and beliefs of our neighbors to name a few.

For example, the principle of using cooperative means to make things better for everyone has been a very simple and logical premise since forever, yet most management in corporations and business cannot see its true significance.

There are a number of different approaches to move us along toward an end game of being virtually moneyfree, and all are viable even if none are a complete solution.

But at the very least, each can contribute towards a workable system in due time whether working alone or in parallel with other means as long as each is contributing to the overall effort of reducing the inefficiency and stress of money and strict accountability at all levels.

Each intelligently planned approach operating alone or together with others could work towards a partial solution leading to an end game of moneyfree global economics

Together they could easily dispose of all money-driven efforts to acquire profit and wealth ordinarily required to achieve a high standard of living anywhere on Earth.

This presentation has several approaches that would ultimately help us to break away from our dependence on the money-driven system, and as such could follow in the order given or in any order found to be prudent.

Providing subsistence basics...

Capping maximum and minimum incomes...

Expanding capabilities of a socialistic economy...

Building a network of modular communities...

Creating a universal monetary system...

Creating a global source of earned money flow...

Now let us imagine how each step along the way could work independently or in parallel in order to accomplish a credible phasing into a universal moneyfree economy.

1 The Concept

The end game would be a moneyfree system where everyone has equal opportunities to pursue happiness and live in freedom and abundance without threat of harm or stress caused by the foibles of profit-driven frenzy.

Considering one approach to moneyfree might entail a logical first step of creating what I define as economic status level (ESL) identity cards similar to social security identification that can be issued to every employed worker.

These cards would define what level of employment each person is presently engaged in and thus account for how their position of employment contributes to the well-being of society by contributing to the common good.

They could be rated in a continuum from unemployed all the way up to work performed at the highest level of qualified contributory value.

ESL cards would be like credit cards in appearance, but would not actually function as a credit card.

They would simply allow access to a computerized system that gave each of them the right, the privilege, the opportunity and the responsibility to perform their work duties free of worry over paying for what their status has included as necessities for subsistence.

~2~

Providing Subsistence Basics

The subject of basics in a moneyfree economy brings in a number of concepts needing a definition relative to some point of reference.

In that light I refer to 'basics' as relative to the word subsistence to mean only the goods and services that the average person needs as a bare minimum for survival.

'Basics' would still be subject to change as the global economy changes to allow additional items, or to exclude some items as being obsolete due to the development of new resources and technologies that make a simple standard of living easy to provide for.

Subsistence basics would be the only items allowed for distribution free of charge to the unemployed, homeless and disabled, and could be defined somewhat differently according to individual needs even though any subsistence items could also be available free of charge to all employed workers regardless of economic status.

A simple economic status level (ESL) card identifying the holder could be issued to all, and checked electronically for every purchase of any subsistence basic to assure that goods and services are given out appropriately in terms of qualified items and quantities.

To be fair, everyone would be automatically qualified for anything defined as a subsistence basic free of charge because the amount of compensation that each worker receives as wages can be adjusted accordingly.

Adjustments would allow for the fact that subsistence items would not require payment and thus add efficiency to how money is regulated for a healthy economic flow.

2 Providing Subsistence Basics

The basic purpose of offering minimum subsistence in terms of goods and services free of charge is to replace the need for unemployment insurance and give anyone who finds themselves unemployed the time and opportunity to find suitable work.

That time and opportunity could open up avenues for new work to suit their skills, interests, training, education and experience thus enabling them to qualify for increased income above the subsistence level.

Another purpose of offering free goods and services for subsistence basics is to recognize that even those who are employed are often workers near or below minimum wage level such as waitresses, waiters, janitors, gardeners, grounds keepers, temporary and part time workers, etc.

Since the number of willing workers in most any society thought of as 'civilized' far exceeds the number of those who try to get through life without working or becoming dependent on others, there is no logical or moral reason why subsistence basics cannot be provided free to everyone whether they are working or not.

The idea of free basics to all has been subtly gaining traction over the last century because of many advances in technology and a steady increase in sheer numbers over the total work force.

Fortunately the result of this revolution in technology is that many goods and services have been made much easier to produce and thus become more readily available for free distribution to the global population.

Logically this makes good sense even without the strict requirement of money paid in exchange despite the fierce resistance by conservatives in government who can't find it in their hearts to sensibly be kind to their fellow humans.

Free subsistence basics make a lot of sense for those less able to make payment to meet normal profit margin costs to uphold strict money accountability.

2 Providing Subsistence Basics

This is evidenced by grocery and department stores that often advertise and offer a plethora of coupons for a vast array of ordinary products to get customers to come in for purchasing many products or services at reduced cost.

Basic subsistence items could easily be set up for free distribution to everyone regardless of income potential, but should be dispensed on an as needed basis and adjusted to individual requirements as best as possible.

All subsistence basics whether they be strictly goods or services for maintaining health or simple conveniences of life could be allocated for free distribution with the only requirement that the dispensation methods would have to keep track of quantities given out to any one person.

To move closer towards a moneyfree economy needs further study to consider the 'value given for value earned' philosophy in order to adjust for the differences between being employed and being unemployed.

With a philosophy of recognition about what the true purpose of money should be, any qualified worker would be looked upon as a contributor to the well-being of the whole and a support for the common good of all.

It would imply that even the minimum wage workers depending mostly upon their free subsistence basics would be allowed to acquire some additional goods and services they qualify for free of charge even if these products or services are somewhat beyond the subsistence level.

With this in mind, any goods and services beyond the subsistence level offered free of charge must be analyzed for consistency with what their employment entails and contributes to the welfare of the common good.

For example, present day waitresses, waiters and all others at or below minimum wage could have their ESL cards identify them as qualified for additional subsistence items for consideration as basic necessities.

Products and services that are normally acquired for a minimum standard of living could be defined as necessities and be included in the definition of all items considered as the basics of life at their employment level.

Using economic status level (ESL) cards, the basics of life for every individual would then be completely free of accountability for such things as groceries, supplements, health foods, clean energy, water, postal service, housing, clothing, telephone, a means of transportation to and from work, basic access to the internet, etc.

Subsistence basics could also include the rudimentary health care everyone needs to maintain a reasonable state of health in supporting themselves and their families and continue their ability to contribute to the common good.

This illustrates the beneficial side effect of avoiding a drain on public resources that quite often happens when impoverished individuals strike out in frustration and turn to crime to express their dissatisfaction with the way they see life is treating them.

As an example of how free subsistence basics can be set up for everyone, let's take a look at the hypothetical life of a typical waitress named Molly.

She had been struggling to pay for the basics at a wage of $2.67/hour plus tips, but was recently issued an ESL card to help increase her overall standard of living with virtually no negative impact to herself or her employer.

By virtue of her employment status card, her manager no longer has to pay her wages beyond a reasonable base salary as a responsible and valued waitress.

As such, she cheerfully performs her daily job with no money worries over the subsistence basics she knows are necessary for the life style she has chosen.

She would no longer require income through tips and the customers are told that tips are no longer expected for her services since she no longer depends upon them.

As long as Molly performs her duties as expected, she should be able to stay happily employed without having to respond to stressful micromanagement activity.

2 Providing Subsistence Basics

Since micromanagement is usually a result of stressful thinking about money issues, the managers of restaurants would not likely have much incentive to apply pressure on their employees as long as their employees do not have stressful money issues themselves.

When she is ready to leave work for home, she does not have to punch a time clock, but leaves assured that she does her work well every day on the job.

On a certain schedule each week she decides it's time to stop off at the supermarket for her week's groceries.

It takes her about an hour to get through the store, fill her grocery cart, and proceed with her selected items for a value checkout.

The first thing she does at the counter is to run her ESL card through the reader to verify her eligibility for a certain level of minimum standard basics.

The products she is purchasing are checked for value and accounted for either as free basics or other products she will pay for at their usual prices.

The checking process totals up both types of items by tagging the basics at no charge and totaling the non-basics for payment out of her personal account.

Molly's card is used in a manner similar to an ordinary debit card to verify that the items she wants to purchase are totaled appropriately in terms of quantity or product type as covered by her card qualification.

Finally the card electronically debits the cost (if any) of her purchase of non-basics from her bank account just like any customer regardless of status.

Groceries are sacked and Molly goes home with her week's worth of food and related items, and goes to work the next day confident that her bills are being met without undue worry of having enough money to cover it all.

As another example, let's say Bill works as a grounds keeper for several corporate offices to ensure that the buildings and grounds are kept clean, lawns mowed and flower beds watered, etc.

Bill's job would normally pay him only at the going rate of $11.00/hour, so up until recently he has had a real challenge to pay all of his bills and sustain his family with the basics he considers as necessities.

Fortunately Bill applied for and was issued an ESL card earlier in the week.

Several of the things Bill has to pay for at his modest residence are his monthly energy cost, water, trash pickup telephone and internet service.

Instead of a corporation, state or federal government thinking they cannot pay more than minimum wage for his job, Bill can now use his ESL card to good advantage to cover what his job and economic status qualifies him for in terms of minimum standard basics.

His employment status card identifies his minimum wage employment level and thus qualifies him to have all of his utilities delivered free of charge.

Since Bill is interested in keeping a clean environment, he also gets online to apply for a free clean energy system involving a revolutionary combination of solar and wind energy conversion units to keep his home heated in the winter and cooled in the summer.

Since his renewable clean energy units are part of the utilities he needs that take the place of systems using fossil fuels, they are qualified for free installation and freedom from payment on any maintenance or replacement costs.

Following suit with his applications for free energy and other utility needs, Bill also applies online to the local trash pickup service for a similar waiver of cost since that is also qualified as a standard basic subsistence service.

Bill and his family use a land line telephone as well as internet access and satellite TV.

Once again, Bill's ESL card grants him and his family free use of these services now considered as necessities of living because Bill is employed at a job considered of good value, and useful to the betterment of society in general.

It doesn't take a rocket scientist or anyone else to see that these examples out of many other scenarios would likely result in win-win situations for everyone concerned.

With adequate money flowing through the economy that neither affects employers nor their workers adversely, a major step toward the concept of 'moneyfree' is in place that illustrates the workings of a system to where business profit and bill payment accountabilities are starting to take a back seat to a more sensible way of living.

These and other examples of using ESL employment status cards illustrate how workers could access the basics of life free of charge in a fair and equitable manner to all

The result would also allow managements to operate without the concern over paying out wages they feel they cannot afford in order to meet their financial obligations.

Free subsistence basics should be a no-brainer for all employers and workers alike when they begin to understand how the system will operate and work to their mutual advantage.

Let us consider some of the side effects when this policy is implemented across the board with no one left out.

With a policy of free subsistence basics in place, the only specifics needed for successful operation are the checks and balances to determine that the system is kept secure from fraudulent use by the unscrupulous.

Consider the likely reduction in various categories of crime when the underemployed, homeless and those living in ghettos finally have access to adequate food, clothing and shelter, and some basic quality medical care .

The effects of a significant reduction in crime also have a beneficial side effect in terms of less money needed for law enforcement, emergency response, and health and medical expense by freeing up funds for other social needs.

2 Providing Subsistence Basics

So with just one social need being implemented (such as this example of providing free subsistence basics across the board), we get a resonant domino effect for improving the welfare of the common good of society in general.

This in turn results in a more efficient economy, more money for education and more money to be paid back in taxes for increasing the beneficial effects of satisfying many social needs spread out over many other areas.

Providing free subsistence basics for everyone could indirectly help provide good jobs and housing for all the homeless and abused women so that their lives could take on new opportunities and positive directions free from the limitations of their previous worries.

As an example of how this step illustrates an important move in the direction of a moneyfree society, it could help generate more contributory citizens to help pay back their dues in taxes for the plan to be self-supportive.

And it seems difficult to dispute that a policy of giving out free subsistence aid to those truly in need is worth a lot more than initial costs might be considered, and a necessary step toward an end game whose time has surely come.

~3~
Maximum and Minimum Income

As long as a socialistic economy is not allowed in the countries where the populace might benefit from one, the mindset that has effectively demonized that idea to rely only on a capitalistic way to do business will continue to suppress and shut out the possibility for free enterprise to allow free basics for subsistence to the needy.

In lieu of that, perhaps the next best thing for moving toward the moneyfree idea would be to define some sensible limits on minimum and maximum income for all wages and salaries to be lawfully defined and independent of the type of employment one is engaged in.

It is logical and reasonable that maximum income for any one person should be capped at a sensible upper limit to reflect the realization that any individual and their family members do not need more money than they can reasonably spend on goods and services for a high standard of living.

Minimum income on the other hand should be capped at a lower limit in order to remain above a reasonable level to substantiate the logic that everyone deserves at least a subsistence income in one form or another.

Therefore the goal for any nation and ultimately for the global economy should be to set a reasonable lower limit for minimum subsistence income and be applicable for every man, woman and child whenever a money-driven capitalistic regime disallows basics to be provided in a compassionate socialistic manner.

For obvious examples, we have the wealthiest in our society right now acquiring billions of dollars in net worth, inheritances, salaries, benefits, perks, dividends, investments

3 Maximum And Minimum Income

and commissions in a continuously unstoppable manner that is apparently incapable of being challenged by anyone with proper authority to do so.

The result is that total net worth of those referred to as the 1% grows way beyond any sensible boundaries needed for optimum living standards.

How fair is it that this monetary free-for-all continues to operate unabated in many countless ways with no one able to challenge the justice and legality of it all?

Is it really fair that many of those less fortunate who for various reasons cannot find sustainable income from their employment are often forced to scrounge and scrape for the money just to pay the bills for subsistence essentials?

America is supposed to be the land of the free and the home of the brave, yet no one finds a reasonable rationale to justify such a struggle in the majority of cases.

Since Congress makes the laws of the land in the United States, why is it not their responsibility to see that just laws are established, and unjust laws are written off?

The answer appears obvious but what has happened for many generations seems in direct opposition to what should be expected of the legislature of the government of the people, by the people and for the people that this nation should not perish from the face of the Earth.

One might ask when the Constitution of that nation was established, why were there no provisions to protect those who for no fault of their own find themselves impoverished and fighting for subsistence when abundance is available for distribution to all and could be provided in a manner fair to everyone based upon their work ethic?

In theory, those at all levels of income, net worth and financial capabilities are supposed to pay proportionately to the tax base so that resources and services are sustained, properly funded and thriving with no tax loopholes to allow legal trickery to avoid giving up their fair share.

3 Maximum And Minimum Income

Unfortunately many who were already wealthy used that wealth to influence politics and those making the laws to slant the rules in their favor.

The end result was that the less fortunate were left with the burden of a significant imbalance of tax obligations that together with improper income forced many into poverty with no effective legal means to stop it.

Ever since the founding of the Constitution, many of us have seen a deterioration of the ability of the average worker to earn a sustainable income and an associated quality of life it was supposed to allow in value given for value earned.

Another way to say it is that because of the capitalistic system that once started out fairly well for the United States in theory; we now see a dramatic breakdown in the ability to maintain fairness for those who cannot get enough money to fight for their cause and a basis for a decent life style.

Many conservatives interpret the freedom and rights of the U.S. Constitution to justify an insidious 'every man for himself' attitude, with the suggestion that those who work hard for long hours to prove their 'worth' deserve to reap the benefits of unlimited abundance and wealth no matter how they happened to get their money.

There's a problem with that.

Simply stated, it says that many of the wealthy do not work hard and long hours to prove their worth, yet still end up far wealthier than most.

Unfortunately many who call themselves conservative tend to buy into a myth that those who are on welfare need to 'get a job and work hard' just like they supposedly did to earn their wealth, and thus blindly write off many who can't work for valid reasons based upon no fault of their own.

Apparently they would like all of us to buy into that same myth that sustainable and adequate income is not for everyone, but only for those who 'prove their worth', and therefore no one else deserves to have abundance or help for the basic necessities if they are already on welfare.

3 Maximum And Minimum Income

Convenient idea, but unfortunately many of the others actually do try very hard and are willing to work hard and long hours but cannot find adequate employment in a land where their Congress withholds federal assistance to create employment with the tired excuse that it 'costs too much'.

Duh squared!

In doing so they refuse to cooperate financially, using a cliché that says it always 'costs too much' to allow funding for creating adequate employment they say has to be created by business and the corporate world, and falsely believe is the responsibility for everyone to find on their own.

Why do they believe this?

Could it be because the wealthy want us all to believe that employment can only be created by business to provide profit for their own coiffeurs and wallets by selling a whole lot of 'stuff' that people may or may not need?

Could it be that they feel they are somehow privileged above the less fortunate who they claim do not deserve help because they (the wealthy) are so good at pointing out the relatively few who abuse the system and therefore complain loudly that welfare abuse is a common condition for most if not all who have been forced to look to welfare to survive?

So how does that argument address the basic questions of not enough available employment for adequate income sustaining jobs and the many related reasons why the lower classes cannot get a leg up financially?

It doesn't address these basic questions at all.

The real solution to the problem needs to be analyzed in the clear light of thoughtful and logical discussions about understanding and addressing the cause of the imbalance.

To reduce the gap between the haves and the have-nots until the difference is adequately reduced and brought under control, those making the laws of the land need to find a way to put sensible limits upon maximum income and net worth no matter what occupation one chooses.

Additional requirements for top salary wealthy and

others considered as the wealthy elite could limit all bank accounts to sensible upper limits to assure that excessive funds could no longer be hoarded, transferred or used in any manner for control purposes.

In the meantime all minimum income levels across the board in any field of endeavor should be raised to the tune of supporting the true basics of life including subsistence groceries, clothing, shelter, clean water, medical care, clean energy, and anything else required to maintain a healthy living standard.

Once limits are established, a maximum income level could gradually be lowered as a minimum income level is raised so that at some point the two levels could stabilize and no longer be a significant problem for the lower class.

Is it not reasonable to assume that any arbitrary upper limits of income can be defined and put into law that are set to assure that such limits are sensible and maintained to the best interest of all parties concerned?

For maximum income, any arbitrary limit should be an amount that is in line to allow purchase of property rights, goods and services that anyone would reasonably need for a definition and acquisition at the high end of a well-earned optimum standard of living.

Any money accrued beyond that limit would seem likely to be used for purposes other than achieving the optimum quality of life including political meddling, influence and attempted control of the actions of others.

The second reason for a logical limit on the maximum income allowed for any individual would be to have it set at a level so that each person is accountable to contribute to the betterment of society in general, and in direct proportion with the philosophy of value given for value earned.

In other words, those who normally contribute the most would be allowed the greatest upper income limit, and those who contribute less due to their employment or willingness to contribute would have their maximum income capped at a lower level accordingly.

Similarly, the limit for a reasonable minimum income level should not go below the criteria to meet and cover necessary basics for subsistence, but could be adjusted upward over time as the cost of most product and service necessities of life become less costly to produce.

Looking at each end of the net worth spectrum, we can easily see that two of the most important problems of the money-driven economy can be solved by setting appropriate limits at both ends.

Regarding the upper echelon of the net worth spectrum, the most serious problem is the unlimited income they are allowed to accrue that invariably leads to some form of corruption, the buying of elections and the suppression and abuse of minimum wage workers.

Corporate CEOs often use their wealth and authority as a power mechanism to suppress and control their employees under the threat of being laid off for no good reason.

These threats are often taken quite seriously and usually become quite stressful to the workers because they know that by being unemployed even for a short time, they might be seriously hurt financially, have difficulty in getting other employment, and be forced to scramble to pay their bills.

At the lower end of the spectrum, the shameful cap on minimum wage has staggered many well-deserving workers from getting an upper hand on their living expenses with the inevitable result of becoming one of the have-nots.

By disallowing any kind of freeze on minimum income, the door would be open to legalize a sensible and adjustable lower limit for insuring that salary and wages must always be no lower than the limit to ensure a reasonable standard for all employees no matter what their field of work may be.

One suggestion comes to mind regarding an appropriate across-the board minimum wage standard for the entire global economy in terms of value given for value earned.

3 Maximum And Minimum Income

That would be having an international agreement to adjust equivalency in minimum income as necessary for changing economic conditions, and have it always adjust upward if technology and resources improve to allow greater abundance to share among all global citizens.

Once set by law, there could be a stipulation that if any responsible business owner or manager cannot meet that level of expense due to unforeseen circumstances, there would be means to apply for economic assistance to assure that necessary funding for minimum wages for all workers can still be met without interruption.

That requirement would put the burden on employers to apply for worker wage expense assistance to compensate for insufficient profits so that employees could continue to work undeterred by concerns over their just dues.

Regarding the other end of the spectrum, much can and should be said and done to assure that the wealthy do not get excessively wealthy by hoarding and taking money out of circulation from an otherwise healthy economy.

No business or political maneuvering should gain the ability to use money for unethical purposes such as asserting power, influence and control over others to do their bidding.

One thing in this regard is to pass an all-encompassing reform setting a strict value cap on all personal net worth coming from any source at a top tier amount that is sensible for assuring that all wage, salary and benefit dispensations are limited for consistency with the agreed upon value given for value earned philosophy.

In addition to wage, salary and benefit caps for income, the international agreement should specify an automatic cap on balances for any bank account to make sure they never exceed a common sense upper limit.

There would need to be proper safeguards to assure that no money could be unlawfully transferred from one account to another or be augmented by additional accounts

3 Maximum And Minimum Income

at home or abroad to contribute to any person's net worth beyond their reasonable limit.

This idea would eliminate all the billionaires' excessive wealth and forcibly drive home the point that no person's net worth should go beyond what is reasonable to achieve everything they would logically need for a top tier quality of life in terms of goods and services.

There are many other suggestions that could put lower limit caps on minimum wages, salary and income as well as upper limit caps on maximum net worth of the wealthy, but whatever ideas prevail, they need to be designed for fairness to all in the international community of nations and cultures.

Putting limits on maximum and minimum incomes that are protected with adequate safeguards is one of the sensible first approach efforts that should be taken seriously in order to move towards the end game of a moneyfree world and a stable international economy.

I suggest that it could set the stage for more ambitious ideas, some of which will be presented in the chapters to follow and will be offered in a manner to hold strictly to the philosophy of value given for value earned in all transactions involving wages and purchases of goods and services.

~4~
Expanding the Social Umbrella

There are socialistic economies that tax their citizens significantly and as a result can give all of their citizens a small range of goods and services without charge.

In spite of that, there are no existing systems that can come close to a true money-free society envisioned by the gurus of the moneyfree concept.

Some of the products and services under the socialistic umbrella offered at reduced cost include college entrance fees, some forms of transportation, some utilities, housing for the otherwise homeless, food stamps, simple means of communication and health care.

One way to analyze social justice in any country is to consider the quality and quantity of welfare assistance each country offers in terms of their ability to provide reasonable economic protection for all in a manner consistent with maintaining a reasonable standard of living without loss of rights or freedoms.

One concept that could move a country in a direction towards a moneyfree concept would be to give incentives to existing governments of each socialistic regime to add to their social umbrella of auto-paid products and services while maintaining fair taxes for everyone.

An equally important step might be for each regime to consider working together with others under a cooperative union of nation states using a common currency and the same totality of goods and services auto-paid by taxes.

Each nation would need to define similar tax rates and offer the same guarantee of rights and freedoms that the most successful governments offer their citizens.

4 Expanding The Social Umbrella

A stipulation would need to be part of the agreement that whatever tax collection method is to be used; it must operate simply and fairly for all including strict negation of any loopholes that the wealthy elite or corporations might take advantage of if they had that opportunity.

This idea could start with a workable time table for the heads of each government to make adjustments to their tax structure to add to their existing welfare umbrella in order to ease the burden of the lower and middle classes.

It could be set up as a cooperative among gainfully employed workers who would not feel negatively affected by paying higher taxes once they are educated about the advantages of a win-win situation for every citizen whether they are defined as being ultra-wealthy, middle class or dirt-poor homeless.

This idea allows the social welfare umbrella to move away gradually from a strict bill-paying accountability with business profit motivation to a more compassionate and logical plan that works for everyone.

With the continued evolution of the global internet moving us towards an automated network of currency and economic record keeping, it might be much easier to get acceptance of the idea of using automatic payment of 'value given for value earned or received' transactions.

Expanding the social umbrella alone does not make a society moneyfree, but it is one good way to get citizens and their leaders to think more along those lines.

This is especially true if nations having similar socially benevolent systems can agree to a unified across the board expansion of their social umbrellas for everyone, whether or not they are gainfully employed, since there is always a plethora of benefits available for the common good that money alone cannot account for.

The idea of a universally automated welfare system set up as an equitable social umbrella is not only theoretically possible, but a logical transition whose time has arrived even for those who have adamantly opposed the idea.

For the many that balk at this idea because of worry over what they perceive as unavoidable human nature of resorting to fraud whenever there is an opportunity, they can eventually put those worries aside.

It doesn't take a rocket scientist to see that it would become increasingly difficult to hack into a computerized system when the motivations of a money-driven system are finally removed and more sophisticated defenses for greater security are developed.

For every hacking offense theoretically possible, there can always be a hacker defense to make it virtually unlikely to compromise any system when reasonably hack-proof systems will become the rule rather than the exception.

Consider a country like Denmark for example.

Let's assume that their present tax rate is 70% to cover certain free goods and services in what could be called a moneyfree cooperative (MFC).

Let's say that this cooperative would include utilities, public transportation, education and health care for all.

By disallowing any loopholes for the affluent to take advantage of so they could reduce their tax payments, the Danish Government could gradually raise the cooperative tax rate giving all citizens time to adjust to changes that in the end add up to significant overall benefits.

No matter what economic level an individual or family starts out in, every responsible citizen could easily see the real benefits resulting from the higher tax rates.

The beneficial effect of increasing the cooperative tax rate would be to introduce more goods and services into the MFC, so that a higher tax is painless and eventually desirable even for the more conservative thinkers.

Every citizen would likely see that since they get a much greater overall benefit from their higher tax rate to cover the necessities of life, the logic of economic trust and cooperation to benefit all really does make good sense as it gradually phases into many beneficial side effects.

Examples of goods and services that could be added to their MFC over time could be additional subsistence food items, clothing, better housing, free utilities including free renewable clean energy, better health care and a basic system for free public transportation.

Other items that could naturally fall into the pot for consideration might include free land line and cell phone service, free postal service and internet access, better vehicles at a lower cost, more vacation and sick pay, less time required on the job, etc.

A planned dynamic of adding additional goods and services to the social umbrella over time could result in a systematic move towards achieving the end game and the ultimate goal of having a lifestyle completely free from the dependence on money and money accountability.

Offered along with this plan for additions to the auto-payment of goods and services would be educational classes for everyone in order to help them adjust to the changes without negative results.

Once tax rates reach an acceptable and sustainable maximum, then additional educational classes could help citizens understand how the increase in efficiency of auto-cost coverage is a win-win solution for everyone.

This is especially true for those of special need and deserving of such benefits, and should be easily observed in the improvements to quality of life for everyone with more freedom resulting from less money accountability.

With ongoing education about the gradual phase into a moneyfree economy, the next generation could be poised to carry on new traditions of not having to account for the money they earn to pay for everything of necessity.

By tweaking the ways in which goods and services can be transformed from a system of bill payment to coverage by a fair tax rate with no loopholes, virtually everything considered a product or a service could be put under the umbrella of a moneyfree cooperative.

The next step for a country like Denmark or any of the other socialistic regimes operating with or without the euro as the standard of currency would be to convince all others to join them in a grand union of countries willing to standardize as many basic goods and services as possible under a sustainable cooperative.

Expanding the umbrella could potentially jump start an enhancement for better global cooperation among all nations and cultures including even the hard core holdouts now seen as immovable adversaries.

If every socialistic leaning nation had an MFC working for their economy, it would negate the need for money exchange for a wide variety of products and services now considered basic for a reasonable standard of living.

By default, a gradual shift from direct payment of bills and accountability for account balances could begin as a nudge of the social umbrella towards a united effort of many nations working together in cooperation and trust.

It would be helpful if every working individual could fulfill their responsibility of supporting a compassionate welfare system that takes away the stigma of welfare fraud.

Thinking differently about money could go a long way towards eventually rendering the need for money as null and void, because manual transactions are being replaced by automatic payment of virtually all products and services throughout a gradually developing global economy.

By tweaking the philosophy of social welfare based upon value given for value earned, a constructive dynamic is brought into play that can eventually force money and all the transactions that require monetary accountability out of the picture to be irrelevant as the necessary medium of exchange.

This would also bring in the beneficial side-effect that the concept and use of debt gradually become outmoded.

4 Expanding The Social Umbrella

The dynamics of credit and debt begin to lose their usefulness while the real essentials of life become vividly displayed for all citizens to see that mutual abundance of goods and services becomes a self-construct reality by way of a globally expanding social umbrella.

It is also realistic to assume that virtually everyone will gladly pay a high rate of taxes (especially if taxes are taken out invisibly), and as a result see the much greater level of benefits they receive to negate traditional worries over bill payments ordinarily stressing their inadequate income.

When a compassionate social umbrella cooperative is set up to eventually phase itself into a totally moneyfree operation when the time is right, the visible results could become a very effective demonstration to the rest of the world that a new way of doing business to end the need of money accountability really does work well by holding to the philosophy of value received for value earned.

~5~
Starting Moneyfree Communities

Is it possible to have well-planned communities that can operate independently off the grid in cooperation and trust and be virtually free of the use of money?

Accountability over paying bills in the modern world of today amidst all the turmoil of politics and fierce religious ideologies seems to be the norm that enslaves us all - yes, even the wealthy elite whether they know it or not.

On a small scale to start with, consider the concept of having a few small communities committed to living only on the basics of subsistence to test the workings of a sensible lifestyle without the need of money or the transactions and accountability of money as we now are locked into.

Think about this way of living as having a potential to evolve and expand into a national and eventually a global network of communities that predominate the economy and operate on a cooperative built on trust and cooperation.

Visualize that you are living in a planned community called Pleasant Valley within a 2500-acre wildlife preserve with an abundance of trees, a confluence of streams, rock formations and hills nestled in a valley of plentiful water supplies, nature trails and grassland making up the quiet surrounding countryside.

Although the idea of living in a moneyfree community does not strictly depend upon such a pristine environment nor even a location situated at ideal latitude and longitude, a well planned community would likely do well to start out with a good choice of location offering relatively stress-free living and the tranquility offered by nature's bounty and peace of mind.

5 Starting Moneyfree Communities

Resident with you in Pleasant Valley are 120 families making up a total population of 450 who are committed to maintaining a self-sufficient mode of life style with an arrangement of modular constructed greenhouses, homes and roadways that serve the needs of the residents without depending on significant help from the outside world.

Your mutual commitment is to live in full cooperation and trust with only the products and services required for subsistence such as adequate food, clothing, shelter and medical care, plus a means of communicating with the outside world to advertise your mode of living.

Most of your food is grown in greenhouses and shared among your residents with the excess stored properly for trade for a few of the necessities you will still need from those who live on the outside, yet are fully supportive and cooperative with your lifestyle.

There is no money exchanged within the confines of Pleasant Valley since all distribution is done with mutual trade of products and services that you and your neighbors have committed to live by and thrive with while testing the operation of a virtually moneyfree society on a small scale.

Everyone in this valley knows that there are a number of other small communities throughout the world that are also operating essentially as moneyfree societies on a small scale due to personal choices and mutual agreement.

Each community is unique, but shares similar concepts that you and your residents have agreed to as part of their philosophy to scale back on previous 'essentials' to allow the moneyfree concept to operate successfully.

Many of these communities are made up of citizens who wish to live outside the grid and be free of the high tech commercial world that placed limitations on creativity and pursuit of the American Dream so often spoken of.

In so doing, they have chosen to rely on their bounties of nature, their work ethics, mutual trust and collaboration while providing documentation on how their practice of

43

being free of money accountability enhances their peace of mind and demonstrates to others how their lifestyle can be applied in many other places.

Existing communities similar to this are not very well known, not advertised and not talked about significantly in the media, but can still operate successfully because their residents make the commitment to live in an environment that sustains healthy living in all the important aspects.

It is typical for the residents to rely mostly upon their own resources and nature's bounty for all the essentials of life, and the standards of healthful living with a minimum of dependency on the outside for products and services to accommodate their lifestyle.

Although these communities are not generally linked together as a united network at the time of this writing, the concept of networking together could easily be a natural for some to allow more moneyfree mode cooperatives to join with them via the internet and thereby expand and increase their participation in numbers and influence.

Doing so would encourage their lifestyle to be better advertised so that others could become educated to the advantages of moneyfree living and become a catalyst for significant change throughout every nation in the global community regarding the true purpose of money.

Networked communities could ultimately provide real reasons to ditch the traditional gridlock of money-driven dependency on capitalism that certain nations and cultures espouse, and in so doing, embrace the new way of doing business that proves beneficial for the common good.

Specifically the new way would be an out-of-the-box mode of thinking that a cooperative moneyfree way of handling transactions really does make sense in terms of the common good it can deliver and maintain for an entire community no matter how large or small it may be.

For every citizen in such a community, it would mean a total commitment to live and operate in full cooperation and trust among all participants so that the responsibilities and methods agreed upon could be applied in any other city, town, state, nation or international community.

The concept of a moneyfree community in any sense should be rooted in the fact that basic needs must be met without unnecessary concerns of financial accountability tied to bank accounts where the balance must never go to zero or below to avoid financial harassment.

Whenever a small community's agreed upon lifestyle allows relatively simple needs for subsistence to suffice, it has been successfully demonstrated that their moneyfree transactions are quite workable for all participants.

Keeping in mind that the word moneyfree is a relative term applicable to a variety of economic interpretations, it becomes possible for each person in these communities to benefit by obtaining their subsistence basics without a lot of stress over monetary accountability.

Theoretically the concept of a high standard of living with no money exchanging hands could take hold in any small community without outside dependency as long as environmental conditions allow and rules of operation are agreed upon by mutual consent of the community leaders given the authority to make that decision.

It is logical to assume that any community successful in establishing their status as a model construct for others to learn from can benefit with additional participants from the outside who arrange to join the community to support the moneyfree concepts already in progress.

Moneyfree communal living can evolve in due time to allow a gradual increase in the variety of available goods and services for addition under a moneyfree umbrella as each successful operation builds upon another.

As communities expand and want to include additional resources for an enhancement to their lifestyle, they can adapt their skills and responsibilities to self-generate more resources or they can remain dependent on outside help.

5 Starting Moneyfree Communities

Eventually these communities can adapt to changing conditions until the time new products and services can be self-generated and added to their communal network, or until other communities join the network to include their resources, education and skills they have to offer.

Beneficial changes can occur gradually over time while communities are still dependent on outside resources for certain products and services that must be purchased with the usual exchange of money and monetary accountability.

Let us imagine that a number of global communities decide they can operate as a network under an umbrella of moneyfree transactions to demonstrate and advertise their status and goals to the rest of the world at large.

Let us say that this network is defined and referred to as a Moneyfree Global Cooperative (MFGC).

An MFGC could allow any other community declaring a similar purpose and commitment the right to join the network on an agreed upon trust and cooperative basis.

Once the network is operational under the designation of an MFGC, other communities may want to study the way it works and decide if they want to be part of it and if so, accept the responsibility of strengthening the network with their skills and resources.

Under this arrangement there would very likely be other individuals, families and businesses that could join an existing MFGC to not only be included in a community of love, compassion, trust and commitment that operates without monetary compensation, but successfully relies on barter and trade for all their practical needs.

Over time, other MFGC networks could be set up to define the necessary designations of goods and services for inclusion under their MFGC umbrella with a commitment based upon 'value given for value earned or received' in regards to all value transactions.

The evolution of every MFGC network that already included everything deemed practical for basic subsistence

46

could adapt as necessary to add to their definition of basics as manpower and changing technology would allow.

Additional products and services would likely become available when new members arrive to offer their natural skills, talents and experience in previous employment with specialized occupations.

Others would likely have access to additional resources such as innovations in electronics, health foods, medicines, tools for construction and advanced technological services previously available only with money transactions and the financial accountability of global economics.

Through internet connection with the world at large, moneyfree cooperatives would become known to related organizations using socialistic philosophies so they could compare their existing operations with other communities having the same purpose in mind.

Any progress being made via the parallel dynamics of moneyfree and social umbrella movements throughout the world are capable of escalating in such a way as to become the wave of the global future despite all efforts to resist it.

The money-driven mindset of status quo economics is destined to systematically fade away and force out the rest of the suppression that has caused all of us to be part of an unnecessary slavery of accountability required in every transaction involved in purchasing products and services we all depend upon for survival.

Each modular MFGC community could network with other communities throughout the world and continue to expand and qualify itself to join up with other networks to create a larger and even more efficient cooperative.

The natural evolution of such an international coop of communities would then become a dominant force behind a benevolent revolution into a pristine world view, even if the concept of moneyfree was the only dynamic at work.

The chances are that once global cooperatives reach a critical mass in terms of numbers, logistics, resources and skilled workers, the global conglomerate of communities would become the main driving force actively at work in producing and distributing products and services for the entire global economy free of charge.

The money-driven world of conservative thinking is sooner or later going to understand that MFGC networks would be unstoppable, and that a revolution whose time had come for installation as an exponential improvement for economic abundance was at hand.

It would not be difficult to observe that a new system of economic abundance and quality of life for every global citizen was working efficiently and securely to close most of the gaps between the haves and the have-nots.

Considering well planned communities for the purpose of testing how well cooperatives can sustain themselves with barter and trade in lieu of monetary transactions would best be located in a friendly political environment.

As evidenced by status quo conservative thinking, any other conditions would leave them open to legal wrangling and potential shut down through oppressive laws passed by unscrupulous political parties in control.

I suggest that locations outside of the United States may work well for starting up an MFGC network including some existing socialistic nations in Europe or similar localities where natural resources are plentiful and climate conditions are favorable for self-sufficiency.

Analysis of a typical community might reveal it to be unique due to location and availability of resources, however there could be an array of products and services available to all other communities regardless of location since each could operate with similar items available everywhere.

Each community could be set up with a stipulation and agreement that anything beyond the subsistence basics and support of their life style could be obtained from the outside through barter and trade when necessary.

5 Starting Moneyfree Communities

Communication with the outside world could be done with the usual telephone, television and internet; however the costs could be paid to the appropriate services operating outside the community with products and services locally offered such as agriculture and other products produced by their skilled workers in trade.

Volunteers within each community would handle all the necessary work of maintenance and reasonable security to insure stable and sustained money free zones that could self-document how well citizens work together over time to cooperate for the common good.

Projects such as these involving communities that agree to operate in a self-sustaining mode would need to commit to an agreed upon lifestyle; yet be open to any necessary modifications, self expansion and networking with other communities for mutual feedback to improve operations.

One important requirement for networking would be access to a modified internet so that if it were the only link with the outside world, it would be sufficient to uphold the moneyfree operations using barter and skilled labor products produced by the community.

Meanwhile, each of these self-sufficient communities operating without monetary transactions could use low-cost advertising to strengthen interest and offer inclusion to all responsible citizens throughout the global community.

In doing so they could offer their usual trade resources to pay for outside advertising to increase their visibility and mutual benefit to all nations and cultures.

As interested parties become aware of the moneyfree communities, there would likely be many who would apply for admission and residence in exchange for their unique skills and work experience.

Continuous immigration to the moneyfree communities would benefit everyone as long as their mode of operation, resources and security systems are maintained without the usual political interference and unethical laws allowed to take precedence and stand in the way of a value given for value earned philosophy.

The agreed upon list of basics for survival in each community could expand as conditions allow for enabling additional products and services to become available as an improved standard of living in the typical cooperative.

This would include skilled labor to build infrastructure, buildings, homes, roadways, and better vehicles for everyday transportation so that the nature and definition of the basics gradually morphs into a balanced evolution of technology and abundance for convenience living.

Essentially there would be two versions of moneyfree living in a global economy, one of which already exists in the form of simple communal living.

This type has existed since time immemorial because our heritage in the modern world began with various cultures learning to live off the land using only their own resources and nature's bounty to provide their essentials.

Starting with that basic idea and expounding on it in a well-planned manner brings in another type of a moneyfree community called technologically engineered cooperatives uniting as a global network.

Communities of this nature would be organized within a global network to become a significant part of an international economic base whose existence is based upon the purpose of creating an eventual phase-over to a totally moneyfree global operation.

Ironically it might take a significant amount of money to start with in order to design and create a global initiative for such a project, but the ramifications of the end game would be enormous and involve a world classroom for educating citizens to the realities of true economic freedom.

The initiative could teach global citizens and the leaders of all nations and cultures how to create and manage a new economic model without the myth that money is a necessity for managing transactions or creating abundance of goods and services to distribute for the common good.

Practical planning for moneyfree community locations would involve choosing sites where adequate water supplies and good natural growth conditions exist so that the primary basics of subsistence living can be found easily.

Considering a typical planned community of this nature, participants could arrange to close out their existing bank accounts, relocate if necessary and install items like clean energy units using solar and wind power technologies.

Other means of support would involve self-sustaining food production using greenhouse growing and sufficient farm equipment to demonstrate the idea that a moneyfree status could last indefinitely and still be flexible to change for enhancements and additional skilled workers to phase in for support and participation.

~6~
The Universal Monetary System

The global economy can be seen as a hodge-podge of monetary systems, many of which work inefficiently when travel and business operations need conversion of currency between various nations.

Still it is a necessity to maintain an easily recognizable and acceptable fairness by having equivalency of value when there are at least two different currencies involved.

The good news is that with the advent of the internet and electronic cybermoney, we have come a long way from the methods of transaction using only coins, paper money, precious metals and other physical tokens declared as having 'value' for the purpose of maintaining equity and fairness according to 'value received for value earned'.

Even though the world of finance involves established complexities we are all familiar with, many of us recognize a need to phase into a simpler system involving electronic currency based upon a universal monetary system.

Doing so could help eliminate many complexities we all know of including visible taxes, interest, credit, debt, stocks, bonds, shares, commodities, credit cards, debit cards, paper money, coins, gold, investments and the whole bit.

Indeed, a sensible transition that some of us have in mind is a totally new monetary system where all money by definition is reduced to the concept of a binary system of numbers maintained and well-secured for transparent access to all personal and business accounts as needed.

Taking it one step further, if all nations, cultures and governments would cooperate and support an electronic money concept that could be referred to as one small step for the global economy, and one giant step for humanity, the result would be a universal currency aptly referred to as the Universal Monetary System being the only accepted system of money qualified for use anywhere on the planet.

The concept itself is not new of course, but the means of defining and getting it established seems very remote to most economists and world leaders because of the usual political logjams of resistance to change, regardless of how sensible the change would be to benefit all.

Ironically, the whole idea of making any kind of change of this magnitude might systematically meet such a fierce resistance from conservatives that it would make a rational consideration of the proposal totally out of the question based upon the usual myth that it would cost too much.

In this case the issue of 'costing too much' would not be the only reason, but would be added to the stumbling blocks of religious and political ideologies that would generate fear of universal money out of mistrust among themselves and seen in other nations perceived to be untrustworthy.

A universal money system would involve defining and implementing a well designed designation of currency in terms of a base unit such as the dollar, a euro or another existing unit chosen for all monetary transactions.

The global system would operate exclusive of all other forms of money for the wealthy elite through the middle class and all the way down to the poorest of the poor in every nation and culture including the 3rd world countries.

Given the fierce combativeness of ultra conservatives that have battled over acceptance of the euro in Europe, it doesn't take a spaceship genius to realize that accepting a change like this would not be easy.

Anything resembling a universal monetary system may require an ultra leap of faith to break through contentious biases of nation against nation and culture against culture so that the time of acceptance of universal currency as the exclusive definition of money has now arrived.

6 The Universal Monetary System

To realize that simple acceptance and the use of universal currency is necessary in order to effectively move forward in a fast changing world is becoming a foregone conclusion by many pragmatists and progressive thinkers.

In fact it has become one of the first steps needed for a well-planned and sensible money system that all nations could use and phase into in order to move towards an end game of universal moneyfree operations that could benefit living standards for every citizen worldwide.

Let us begin the logic and rationale of considering an exclusive currency system with a commitment to think about the true purpose of money.

Visualize how it would look and operate by referring to it simply as the universal monetary system.

By design it would have to have many ramifications that could encourage simplicity and lead to better quality of living by reducing concerns over monetary transactions.

As a precursor to a true moneyfree system, it would be a feasible first step towards the ultimate goal of how the global economy should operate.

Let us assume this system has some ramifications we can group under one name as a structure for economics consisting of seven subsystems working together for the benefit of all in a global network.

As a suggestion for suitable terminology, let us refer to it as the Socially Automated Network Economy (SANE), consisting of seven subsystems having specific purposes as necessary to work together under one name.

The SANE economic model would not be designed as a capitalistic based system nor would it be a modification of a traditional socialistic doctrine, but would be a logical and compassionate mix of the best of both systems in order to operate fairly and equitably for all citizens.

With all seven subsystems efficiently working together as one unified concept, the result would be the elimination of all antiquated money concepts that have complicated the quality of life for most throughout past generations.

The start up idea of SANE as I have envisioned would totally eliminate the use of paper money, coins, credit and loans, monetary conversions, visible taxation, speculations, checking accounts, stocks, bonds, investments, coupons, food stamps, gold, silver, other precious metals, bit coins and anything else traditionally used for money.

All transactions would involve the use of the universal monetary currency recorded electronically and redundantly secured in a simple unification of records kept throughout the world so that no matter how trivial any transaction is, it would be documented for accessibility and transparency to any qualified account holder.

To accommodate citizens in 3rd-world countries and others who could not easily transition into an electronic management system, there could be the temporary use of coins and paper money for later conversion to electronic currency when these citizens have had sufficient time for education on using electronic money for their transactions.

For personal and business purposes it would be an easy task to produce portable electronic devices similar to cell phones and referred to as Electronic Currency Tablets (ECTs) for displaying all monetary transactions whenever needed for reference to their account holdings

The idea envisions that virtually everyone would want easy access to a personal ECT for the purpose of keeping track of their account balances as a result of changes any transaction would make regardless of how great or trivial the amounts would be.

In doing so, it would electronically display account ID and any changes to their balance of currency whenever a transaction for purchase of goods or services is dispensed.

This vision of a universal monetary system as the basis of SANE economics would need to be well planned and designed to eliminate or significantly reduce the possibility of any fraudulent transfer or usage of funds.

It would have to be designed so that every transaction is recorded, documented and stored in a global network of locally operating branches using secured funds in a hack proof cyber system of redundant checks and balances that is fully transparent for online verification.

Each local bank would record any transaction and the identity of all participants for comparison with stored data that could be redundantly available at any other local bank in the network for a virtually foolproof security procedure in case of loss of records at any one location.

All transactions could be validated with the knowledge that the system would disallow any data to be lost, stolen, compromised or manipulated in any fraudulent manner.

To give additional assurance to all account holders, there should be a strict stipulation that all funds would be insured for replacement against any kind of loss in case this unlikely event would actually occur.

As a result, all monetary transactions could always be accessed and redundantly traced to any individual or event involved with any transaction at any location throughout the entire global network.

Since money would still exist and be the tool for all transactions in a SANE based economy, it would continue to be the driving force throughout the global system and still be vulnerable in terms of one problem that could not be totally eliminated by using hack-proof cybermoney.

This would happen in any money-based system and would likely occur since the system would not likely be set up to stop the transfer of money from one individual to another, or from one business to another in ways that go against the philosophy of 'value given for value earned'.

So even though SANE economics would be a giant leap forward in the path towards a moneyfree existence, as long as money was still the means of operation in the economy, it could not function totally free of fraudulent use and reach the true state of moneyfree all by itself.

Not to worry, because I see the SANE system as an evolving system and a necessary step forward that would position the global economy to maneuver itself and the entire socioeconomic environment to a level never before matched by any systematic change of this magnitude.

Fortunately it is still human nature for most of us to strive for the finer things in life in an ethical manner.

By doing so with the knowledge that cooperation and mutual trust can go a long way for enabling personal goals to be realized, the SANE economic model could introduce the advantages of a significantly moneyfree way of doing business that is easily adaptable to new innovations.

Indeed it could prove itself manageable in a relatively short time and create orders of magnitude better efficiency in production and distribution of all necessary products and services in a fair and equitable manner.

So even though complete assurance against fraud and other crime is not guaranteed with SANE as I envision it to start with, the motivation for most individuals to better themselves through a reasonable work ethic would be the significant rule and not the exception.

In a SANE based global financial arrangement, most everyone would understand that raising their own standard of living happens easily and quickly when most citizens put out reasonable efforts in personal contributions for the benefit of the common good.

In this effort they would be automatically experiencing a win-win situation for themselves and everyone else.

To illustrate a plan for converting all of the world's currency into a new medium that is now referred to as cybermoney, it is logical to offer incentives to help counter the inevitable resistance of many nations' leaders.

An adequate incentive should be given to all nations and cultures to think about the advantages of the plan so that public education illustrating the ramifications of a universal monetary system could be better understood.

Let us start with a logical suggestion that has a sound basis by defining a unit of currency that could be used for universal acceptance and function in a manner similar to how bitcoins are used today.

But unlike a bitcoin system, all account holders would have full access and control with the transparency needed to view their accounts at any time.

They would need complete assurance that hack-proof security measures are in place and that full accountability at each local branch of the banking system is guaranteed.

Adequate means to prevent fraud or errors created by the system of account managers would need to be well-planned, stipulated and completely explained to the public of every nation using easily understood terminology and assurance of security in all personal account information.

Every account holder would be able to verify that their accounts were accessible and available for inspection at any time with easy capability for corrections if necessary.

Let us assume that a unit of universal money is defined by the term **sharo** (singular or plural) instead of a dollar or a euro, having a fixed value equal to the approximate value of one dollar or the value of any other accepted unit taken at the trade value at time of conversion.

The idea would be to have every cyber account in the system work only in converted values of **sharo**, with the total number of **sharo** issued to each account set equal in value to existing account values at the time, plus a fixed amount as a reward given to every account holder for accepting the challenge of thinking about money in a new and exclusive system of unit amounts.

For example, the fixed amount added to all accounts globally might be designated as 15% which would then be available to help pay off existing debts that many account holders might have in today's money manipulations.

6 The Universal Monetary System

To construct the universal money system to be even more efficient in everyday transactions, a logical rule could be defined to disallow any fractionalization of units.

Instead, pricing for all transactions in payment for any product or services would deal only with whole numbers of **sharo** using simple adjustment of prices and wages to go up or down to the nearest whole number of value for greater ease in accounting.

All prices of goods and services for each nation would need to be converted into the approximate equivalency of value that each nation's currency had previously defined in their everyday transactions.

Wages, salaries and payments for employment and any other dispensation to individuals would use the same logic by converting previous currency into equivalent values of **sharo** for payments in line with the philosophy of value given for value earned.

~7~
The ShareFlow Money Pool

As long as we rely upon a money-driven economy, it seems that if we are to have an exceptional overhaul of the financial world, it should begin with what I call the first of seven subsystems of the SANE economy.

By definition I choose to call it the ShareFlow Money Pool or simply ShareFlow set up as a global money base using electronic cybermoney as the universal standard.

ShareFlow would be set up to have every other form of currency converted into just one standard medium of exchange that would reside within a secure world bank management system to handle all monetary transactions.

The system would need to be the agreed upon source of secure money universally available for all transactions and would be maintained by a computerized electronic network accurately qualifying and quantifying all input and output for any monetary transaction.

ShareFlow would have to be designed and created to operate with secure transfer of funds from one account to another, and be controlled as the only designated money system for all global operations.

In doing so, it would be set up as a networked banking system with local branches capable of being redundantly operational in all global localities for transactions between individuals, businesses and governments.

The rule of operation would be to never allow credit, debt, account deficit or operational errors of acquisition in funds to occur, and as such would only allow transfers of a qualified number of monetary units (previously defined as **sharo**) for intended purposes.

8 Minimum Standard Income

ShareFlow would not operate with the use of credit or the issuance of loans requiring interest and payback on debt for any business, personal or government account.

With ShareFlow as a universal money pool originally conceived for flat tax rates from wages and purchases of goods and services, it could now be redefined as a new basis of operation for an enhanced SANE economy.

It could operate without the need for taxation by using a method of direct transfer of money from one account to another that will be explained shortly.

The SANE economic philosophy in its entirety would be to help relieve the stress about having sufficient money to pay bills and taxes, and as a result would always respond with qualified funding available to anyone with legitimate needs without requiring visible taxation.

With ShareFlow phased in as the basis of the SANE economy, there would be no need for visible taxation of any type since all wages and purchases of products and services could now involve direct transfer of funds from a personal or a business account into or out of ShareFlow for an efficient money flow throughout the economy.

In effect, this would be a vastly more efficient means of transferring cyber-currency, since all accounts would exist within ShareFlow as being the only source of money qualified for legitimate transactions.

Essentially ShareFlow could be considered equivalent to an infinite source of funds for distribution as required for qualified purposes including the basis of creating jobs and funding wages for employment and entrepreneurship throughout the global economy.

ShareFlow would be the only necessary and universally available source of money needed to support a continuous supply and healthy flow of funding for any qualified need throughout the world economy.

As previously defined, the cyber unit **sharo** would be the only qualified unit of cybermoney necessary to make financial accountability an easy process for any nation to adhere to in a standardized manner.

ShareFlow could be designed and automated to always respond fairly, efficiently and proportionately to the needs of the entire extent of the world's population for any and all legitimate purposes without exception.

The simple purpose of the universal ShareFlow money pool would be to enable qualified transfers of universal cyber-currency from any pre-qualified personal or business account in the global economy to any other pre-qualified account also residing in ShareFlow.

All universal money would flow throughout the global economy according to the legitimate acquisition of wages and payment for purchases based upon a 'value received for value earned' philosophy for any individual, business, corporation or government of any nation.

I see the system as disallowing any form of deficit or spending on credit to create any form of debt or excess of funds in any account whether it is a personal, business or a government account set up for government operations.

There would never be any lending or credit required since the philosophy and goal of the ShareFlow banking system would be to fund all accounts adequately and fairly by always using the principle of giving value only for value earned in a way that contributes to the common good.

This philosophy could be used as the foundation of future banking and operate without the need for anyone to make future payments on any purchase by using credit or paying off a loan as is the common practice in virtually all existing methods of financial planning.

All social services including funds for education, the basics of food, clothing, shelter, healthcare, transportation, utilities, means of communication, etc. could be provided according to the priorities of human need.

With ShareFlow, credit would never need to be issued or used in any way since the system would have a variety of specific funding programs available for the necessary basics without allowing any individual, business or agency of the government to go into debt.

Everyone would be paid automatically and adequately for wage and salary income payments and be debited fairly for purchases of goods and services no matter what their status in life might be.

With the only source of funds being securely managed by ShareFlow working in conjunction with the rest of the SANE subsystems, there would never be out-of-balance conditions traditionally recognized as inflation, recession, depression or other economic concerns.

As a result, there should always be adequate funding and correct accountability for every transaction whether it is in the form of salary income to the gainfully employed or simply paying a bill for products or services.

The payment of funds directly back into ShareFlow for purchases would be in lieu of visible taxation since all purchases would automatically include amounts normally associated with sales tax and allow the money pool to be managed as an all inclusive universal banking system to support a holistic social services network.

It would operate securely to maintain efficiency, trust and cooperation between all nations for the continuation of economic justice for all their citizens.

ShareFlow would be designed in such a way as to have the entire system set up for peaceful purposes only which would disallow funding for foreign war efforts or political corruption processes at any level.

All social service programs would have online access to funds from any local ShareFlow management office and have redundant record keeping at all other locations.

This would assure simple but secure electronic funding for completing any transaction according to the principles of adequate security, qualification, and fairness according to the priorities of human need.

Large expense items such as homes and cars could be purchased on lease requiring no interest payment, with the definition of debt not applicable using periodic payments; since it is more logical to pay for the gradual use of any large ticket item over time instead of direct ownership.

Everyone in the global economy could be paid wages, salaries or other payments they have rightfully earned by receiving qualified periodic input into their accounts from ShareFlow for any form of employment performed legitimately.

The mechanics of actual transfer of funds for payment involving goods and services could use portable electronic currency tablets (ECTs) or alternately rely on debit cards that anyone could carry similar to an ordinary credit card.

Businesses would use either a portable ECT or a larger business machine set up that performs the same function but is physically fixed and available at the place of business such as cash registers would be.

The function of either device would be the same and simply set up to perform two types of operations.

In one case, there could be a qualified number of wage units dispensed from employer to employee for a periodic wage dispensation, salary allocation, or a consulting fee payment on a set time schedule.

At the time of transfer, funds from the employer's business account residing in ShareFlow would transfer to the employee's personal account also in ShareFlow so that the employee receiving his or her wage payment would not have to deal with income tax because ShareFlow would have all the money considered as taxes paid automatically through the sale of products and services

For customers purchasing a product or service from a business, a similar procedure would process transactions involving the required funds to transfer from a customer's personal account in ShareFlow to the business account of the store or other facility offering the product or service.

8 Minimum Standard Income

All monetary transactions would be simple transfers from one account to another within ShareFlow, since the ShareFlow system would be the only banking system in existence set up to maximize convenience and efficiency for smooth flowing operations throughout the economy.

With complete transparency of operations, ShareFlow would become a trusted overseer for self-management of legitimate transfer of funds from one account to another because it would be set up as a universal money pool of infinite capacity and would not need a strict accountability of the totality of funds within itself.

The real function of ShareFlow would be to manage the legitimate transfer of funds from one account to another without the requirement of having citizens be accountable in taxes for contrived indebtedness ingrained in our beliefs that money cannot be shared for the common good but must always be paid back to the soul-less system that created it.

ShareFlow would have a virtually infinite capacity to dispense and accept whole number amounts of **sharo** to be used for any and all monetary transactions of any type in a transformed global economy based upon the simple philosophy of value given out for value earned or value needed for qualified future operations.

The actual quantity of **sharo** in ShareFlow could be accounted for theoretically, but the necessity for trying to hold to a specific balance would no longer be necessary since there would be no debt or debt ceiling in existence.

ShareFlow's function would have the sole purpose of managing all input and output totals of **sharo** transferred between the various personal, business and government accounts contained within ShareFlow itself.

In essence, ShareFlow would 'own' all the money in existence, but that would be a good thing since 'owning' and managing the accounts would end up being the same thing in order to function without loss of rights or freedoms by any of the citizens.

As such, all traditional forms of money management would disappear including all forms of accountable taxes, credit, interest, debt, brokerage, investments, speculations, currency exchanges, gold, silver and other precious metals and minerals, paper money, checks, credit and debit cards, coupons, coins, stamps and …(pun intended) – including the whole bit-coin.

All occupations involving unusual attention to money and money accountability would phase out and disappear including financial advisors, investment brokers, private bankers, the IRS, the Federal Reserve, political campaign managers, over-paid politicians, ultra wealthy attorneys, CEOs, over-paid sports and entertainment stars, insurance brokers, casino operators, etc.

All accounts would be savings accounts since there would be no need to have a checking, trust or any other account type with all funding sources held safely and securely within ShareFlow.

One idea for convenient purchasing at retail outlets could have customers carry personal monetary value cards that have been 'charged up' at home by using an app that activates their cards to a set value for limited purchases.

This allows their card to have a temporary limit placed upon purchases to avoid undue concerns of vulnerability to loss or fraud regarding their net worth in ShareFlow.

As an example of ordinary purchases of groceries at a supermarket, let's look in on a typical customer Jeff Martin who has just come up to the check stand with his basket of groceries for the week.

Jeff does not have to deal with a credit card, a check book, coupons or any other means of complication to pay for the items since he can hand the monetary value card to the cashier who would validate his identity and then run it through to debit the total cost in an easy one-step fashion.

Groceries would not have any sales tax add-on, or use

coupons since all products have fixed pricing without any in-store advertising for specials.

The store where Jeff shops for groceries would not be relying on profit to stay in business since there would be adequate financial arrangements within ShareFlow as part of the SANE economy that allows businesses to no longer rely on profit to operate successfully.

The store gets adequate operational funding through ShareFlow by way of an auto-deposit method of putting funds into the store's business account on a regular basis based upon their track record of previous operations.

All employees of the store including the management and owners would get paid according to their status as a worker, and at appropriate rates commensurate with their employment value to the common good.

Payments to employees would be in monthly deposits from the store's business account held in ShareFlow.

Since business and corporate accounts would be part of the global ShareFlow financial system, they would have to be accessed independently of personal accounts so that funds are deposited only to appropriate accounts, and in a manner consistent with value given for value earned.

Business accounts would not be allowed to transfer money into their personal accounts, since the purpose of business accounts would be to pay salaries and any other legitimate business expenses.

As another example, let's say that Margo Johnson is manager of a new corporation called WindStream that produces renewable clean energy generators by using wind power to generate electricity.

Similar to any other business account, her corporate account would have subdivisions for several purposes, one of which would be for purchasing necessary materials for use in constructing the company's products.

Margo puts in an order for a shipment of rotors that are produced by another company, and then pays for the shipment out of WindStream's business account.

Like any other business, WindStream will get funded automatically by virtue of their success as a business and in periodic income payments quantified as a function of their projected expenses justified by past performance.

Since even government accounts would be managed and funded by ShareFlow, agencies such as the IRS and Federal Reserve would no longer exist.

Instead there would be responsible management teams within ShareFlow set up to direct necessary government money to fund all projects approved of by the majority of citizens.

Government accounts would no longer need tax funds or profit through sales or foreign trade, but would be paid their necessary funding as a function of qualified expense projections for various accounts.

Each government account would be a subdivision of a total value account managed by ShareFlow so that all input and output involving account values would be managed in a manner consistent with the philosophy of value given for value qualified for present and future operations.

Congress would no longer be allowed to stop a release of funding for projects approved of by the people since ShareFlow would have all the money in existence so that all government agencies would be constrained to operate ethically and morally by attending to their true prescribed duties of passing laws approved by a majority of citizens

ShareFlow would have adequate funding for any and all social programs and a reasonable level of foreign aid to qualified countries that do not advocate resorting to war in lieu of sensible negotiations to resolve conflicts.

To summarize, the ShareFlow banking system would revolutionize the way money is thought of and used, and could include options for allowing personal accounts to have subdivisions, possibly one for input, another for high end purchases, another for medium value purchases and one for everyday transactions as an example.

Business and corporate accounts could also be broken down into separate subaccounts such as one for business purchase of products, one to pay for non-salary services and one for wage and salary dispensation.

All business and corporate accounts would now be non-profit and be funded according to their track record of success in operating for the common good.

Government accounts could also consist of divisions within their total value accounts, such as one for purchases of products, one for wage and salary payments to workers, one for legitimate foreign aid, and one for state and local dispensation of essentials approved by the citizenry.

Campaign expense accounts would need to be limited but funded equitably by having only one for each qualified candidate running for each office so that each candidate is confined to that money alone for use in their campaigns.

Only equitable value accounts would be allowed for use in political campaigns since there would no longer be PAC funds, corporate, business or any other huge donor contributions allowed from any source.

~8~
Minimum Standard Income

With a well-planned ShareFlow Money Pool system in operation, all welfare programs could be easily replaced with a Universal Minimum Income Program (UMIP) that would act as the foundation of a much needed overhaul of our much maligned welfare systems we have going today.

The UMIP would provide for every man, woman and child to have unconditional basic income for subsistence whether or not they are gainfully employed.

Funds could be transferred directly from ShareFlow to their ShareFlow personal accounts typically on a regular basis like monthly payments from Social Security.

It would be subsistence income intended to cover the costs for the necessities of survival only such as reasonable quality and quantities of food, clothing, shelter, healthcare, and other related products and services and would be a basis of personal income whether employed or not.

Equal allocations would be available to everyone to insure fairness to all and would need to be allocated in a secure way and be accompanied with positive incentives for everyone who is able to do useful work to contribute with meaningful employment for the common good.

Even though minimum income could be issued equally to everyone no matter what additional income is earned through employment, the actual rates for issuance could be adjusted according to variations in the economy.

Since every citizen would be getting equal payments of free money for subsistence items only, it must be managed in such a way that the system can easily maintain a balance by making periodic adjustments to the UMIP to assure that money continues to flow equitably and freely through the global economy without undue stress or concern over perceived national debt, inflation or recession.

With this arrangement of the ShareFlow Money Pool using a universal monetary standard I have arbitrarily defined in terms of electronic cybermoney called **sharo**, visible taxation would no longer be applicable.

Every purchase of goods and services would pay the entire bill directly to ShareFlow which could pay wages directly to all citizens according to their qualification of employment status contributing to the general welfare of many and the common good of all.

Businesses would also be reimbursed by ShareFlow directly as a function of the number of qualified workers employed by the business, seeing to it that no employee would be getting underpaid or overpaid

With this arrangement, everyone still has to manage their accounts whether they have a personal or a business account, but no one uses credit or goes into debt.

It seems that anything giving free goods and services to anyone is ultra-radical thinking for conservatives and also disparaged by many called middle-of-the-roaders.

All employed workers would receive their fair share of free subsistence income allocations in addition to income they earn through gainful employment.

In the strictest sense everyone would be on 'welfare' for subsistence basics only, however the system would be funded adequately through invisible 'taxation' paid back to ShareFlow from every purchase of products or service.

Although the UMIP could be referred to as universal welfare, the recipients would not have to carry the stigma opinionated by many conservatives who claim that most welfare recipients are simply lazy loafers who need to 'go out and get a job' to earn a living.

As we all know, it is traditional for most capitalists to want to go ballistic over any remark suggesting support of even a hint of a welfare or socialistic state, but if everyone is on the welfare payroll, it becomes a bit more difficult to present a credible argument against it.

What they fail to recognize is that times have changed dramatically from the days when everyone lived in harsher physical conditions, limited technologies and did not have the ability to take advantage of labor-saving systems.

Economic evolution now make it possible for an over-abundance of products and services to be easily produced so that every human on the face of the Earth could have access to the basics of living and much more.

Conservatives fail to realize that thinking outside the box they were raised with and passed on from generation to generation should have allowed them to dispose of fixed mindsets that became archaic and inevitably stood in the way of progress that could have benefited everyone.

By changing the system that provides the logistics for delivering the basic essentials, we can remove the stigma of unfairness promoted by many conservatives who claim that 'hard work' is always necessary to survive and that it is 'quite impossible' for differing cultures to work together to cooperate for the benefit of all.

Short of a switch to a full-blown money-free society, as long as the money-driven quagmire is the rule of the day, the UMIP could be the most significant manifestation of improved efficiency and fairness attributable to any economic structure and be called an important baseline of the Socially Automated Network Economy (SANE).

Set up properly, it would replace the hodge-podge of traditional welfare and charity organizations with a basic minimum standard that could go global in scope so that no culture or nation would be left out.

The benefits of this concept would be potentially jaw-dropping to some, but far-reaching and beneficial to everyone and could result in having every man, woman and child on Earth be in position to share the abundance of life naturally and rightfully available to all.

An abundance of products and services available to all should be a God-given right and one that should rightfully be respected and equitably maintained without exception.

Contrary to popular conservative beliefs, the idea of a minimum standard income for all would turn out to be the result of a basically simple idea to implement.

It is clear that sensible and efficient financing is now possible for everyone because all money can now consist of electronically arranged bits in a secure banking system that defines amounts and balances for any existing account no matter where it is or what currency is used.

Minimum standard income can take the form of any means that can successfully deliver it to those who deserve it, and even though the concept is designed especially for raising minimum wages for the lower classes, it can work equally well for anyone with no adverse effects.

The program would have the ability to integrate fairly with all levels of employment regardless of wages and net worth of those who could get by without it.

For many, the UMIP would be an idea whose time has come, and would logically work better than any hodge-podge of welfare systems now in existence.

The UMIP set up properly could dispose of thinking that it would be totally unworkable or too radical, and thus be aggressively attacked by many conservatives who like to feed this way of thinking to their constituents and others.

With the entire SANE concept in operation, virtually everyone could and would likely want to gravitate to a favorable job opportunity of high contributory value since the underlying nature of most humans is to search for a way to better one's station in life.

As a result, it doesn't take a proverbial rocket scientist to show how and why a minimum standard income would be a logical means of providing an equitable maintenance of subsistence income available to all.

The UMIP would have a convenience of delivery and a means to maintain a reliable system without depending upon contributions of visible taxes paid by wage earners or taken out of the purchase of goods and services, since ShareFlow would be self-manageable without any of that.

Because of the built in security and efficiencies of ShareFlow in general, any nation or culture could be more than happy to support their so-called 'welfare state' based upon cybermoney, since it could prove itself successful by example not only for the unemployed, but also for all employed workers independent of where they are located.

The UMIP need not be referred to as socialism per se because it would actually amount to a whole new form of workable economics that allows the best principles of a capitalistic economy to remain alive and stay well.

By getting beyond the stigma of semantics, it would be closely aligned with a different system that might rightfully be called a compassionate socialism working for everyone.

The premise of understanding and embracing the true meaning of 'compassionate' is meant to emphasize that no one loses any of their rights or freedoms by accepting the realization of what the term 'socialism' is all about.

The idea of a SANE economy as I will illustrate, might be a monumental leap away from any traditional form of socialism managing to survive amidst all the harsh and ill-placed criticism in existence today.

The UMIP would be fair to all since every employed worker would get a standard minimum income base plus any rightfully earned income in addition to that; while the unemployed for whatever reason would receive only their base minimum payments they would have to use wisely to live on as long as that was their only income source.

For the relatively few who are capable of working but for some reason find an excuse not to would be forced to use their base minimum income to purchase all the bare necessities of living, including food, clothing, shelter and basic health care.

Minimum standard income payments would be issued only for essentials and would electronically disallow any purchases of anything except qualified goods and services.

With UMIP, there would have to be a strict stipulation to disallow loopholes that might allow anyone to sidestep the system or take advantage of the program fraudulently.

All payments issued from ShareFlow would need to respond to hack-proof coded information on all personal and business acquisitions at the point of transaction.

This security arrangement would have to disallow any transfer of money exceeding amounts authorized, or for purposes other than the acceptable amounts approved for purchase of qualified products and services.

~9~
Comprehensive Insurance

The next of seven subsystems of the SANE economy I see as vitally necessary would be the inclusion of a long-awaited all-encompassing system of universal insurance.

I see no reason why it could not cover all the priorities of life including basic health care for every person, plus reasonable coverage for household pets to cover expensive veterinary bills of medical necessity.

Yes, even household pets should be included as a basic need for living in our day and age where the well-being of dogs, cats and other pets has become a priority for many.

The requirement of an all-inclusive insurance to exist in a money-driven economy needs to include the fact that adequate resources should be made available to educate users and fund providers for all reasonable needs.

For healthcare alone we need to have an across the board increase for additional doctors, nurses, technicians and other health care specialists needed for comprehensive care plus the proper equipment they need to make such a bold venture a sustainable reality.

Health care would need to go far beyond all the things the Affordable Care Act intended, although creation of the ACA was a good step in the right direction to help replace the hodge-podge of inadequate insurance systems that existed at the time it was put into law.

Truly the existing insurance plans at the time left much to be desired for their lack of efficiency and availability that effectively forced medical care to be unaffordable for the average citizen who had the right to sustainable health care coverage without exception.

9 Comprehensive Insurance

It is ironic that automobile and other motor vehicles are required by law to have adequate coverage to protect the public from the ravages of traffic accidents that result in property losses, loss of life and serious injuries, but only recently was a similar effort put out (via the ACA) that required every citizen of the United States to have a basic level of health care coverage.

For quite some time, laws of the land required that the public needed to be protected from death and injury by vehicles, but there was no law established for the purpose of protecting them from death, injury or illness as a result of not being covered by health insurance.

Can anyone seriously deny that there must have been something wrong with that picture?

This then bodes a logical question: Why not have a sensible law in effect that allows all types of insurance to be made available and affordable for every reasonable and legitimate purpose?

And why not have it so affordable that it would cover everyone regardless of income capabilities and be offered without penalty for non-compliance?

ShareFlow could be set up to include authorization for the distribution of insurance funds for whatever qualified purpose is identified as a legitimate priority for coverage.

In other words, why not have every existing insurance company throughout the nation (and eventually through-out the world) be replaced with one system to be operated as a universal insurance program supported by ShareFlow?

A Universal Insurance Program (UIP) would be the logical means to operate in such a way as to be essentially automated, cost effective, sustainable and complete for covering all legitimate insurance needs.

And since I am suggesting that we take that grand leap out of the punitive mindset of conservative thinking, why not have it include all types of insurance needs from the least to the greatest, and put them all under one efficient and well secured management system?

For healthcare coverage it should include accident, life, major medical, disability and preventive care.

For general coverage it should include theft, loss of property, weather and climate change disruption, and any other types of coverage for loss having a priority need for financial reimbursement.

Similar to the philosophy of the Universal Minimum Income Program, the UIP would be a subsystem of SANE for being organized intelligently, responsibly and fairly to cover and facilitate all legitimate compensations and claims of any nature on a priority basis.

There would be no loopholes or legalities to have any coverage withheld as is often done with existing insurance companies who want to disallow payments on the basis of technicalities tied to protecting their profits.

As a vital part of the SANE economy, the UIP would compensate for all claims reasonably, equitably and fairly for every type of insurance qualified as part of a hierarchy of the priorities of human need in order to maintain and support a reasonable quality of life for all.

UIP's philosophy would be to cover all the important needs first, but still be responsive to all other claims on the basis of ability to respond with the specific resources and technical assistance available at the time a claim is made.

To fulfill every legitimate claim equitably and fairly at all times makes the assumption that the proper resources, skilled workers and facilities are always available.

Since we live in an imperfect world, even UIP could not always guarantee 100% response and coverage for all claims in every situation, however it would be set up as a non-profit dynamic for self-improvement at all times.

For optimum universal healthcare alone, preparations for the UIP to handle reasonable coverage for everyone in an automated fashion would require continuous release of adequate funding from ShareFlow for the ongoing training of medical personnel as needed.

This of course would include many physicians, nurses, dentists, specialists and the technical assistants required to fulfill the needs of a continuously expanding demand for coverage with a level of respondents who would always be available at every hospital, urgent care and other medical facilities for responding properly in a global environment.

While medical personnel are being trained to come up to speed at the time of the UIP launch, there would also be the need for adequate funding from ShareFlow to build additional hospitals and other medical facilities as well as manufacturing and distribution of all medical equipment that such an expansion of demand would require.

The idea would be to pre-plan projected needs across the board that would include support equipment for every medical facility to maintain existing personnel and others they would need for handling the increase in services.

Since ShareFlow would be an all-inclusive money pool for virtually any qualified need; then as long as conditions and manpower are not limiting factors, every citizen could expect that virtually all of their legitimate needs would be covered in a reasonable manner by virtue of the free flow output of funding from the universal monetary system.

The UIP would be set up to abolish all the wasted and duplicated effort, red tape and the illogical bureaucracy of hassling over claims that thousands of competitive plans in operation still do to this day.

The UIP would open up a surprisingly more efficient way to handle medical claims since there would no longer be the need to account for who is covered and who is not, or what is covered and what is not in a manner consistent with reasonable intent and available resources.

All claims would be processed and paid as necessary on a priority basis, with some being paid automatically by virtue of funding directly from Share Flow.

9 Comprehensive Insurance

All non-trivial needs would be covered and satisfied in a timely manner assuming that the global environment does not have too many resource depletions all at once.

If any service center supported by the UIP became overwhelmed by the lack of trained personnel, resources, facilities or damage due to unforeseen events; contingency plans could be in place to divert resources from one place to another to better handle the emergencies and get local operations up and running again as soon as possible.

The tired old cliché called 'lack of money' would no longer be an issue in the SANE economy since ShareFlow would operate automatically to fund all qualified purposes without having to account for a debt ceiling, adequate tax payments or any other funding dependency at the point of service normally associated with service breakdown.

If something like a catastrophic natural disaster that affected millions did happen, then a prioritized schedule of compensations would have to be re-evaluated according to an updated priority response plan.

When natural disasters and global conflicts are at a minimum, it would allow more funding to qualify for use on the lesser impacting considerations.

That would allow for educating a potential surplus of workers and greater production of equipment and facilities to be put on reserve in anticipation of future hard times.

This variance would occur from year to year, however since all money would be sourced from just one banking system called ShareFlow, funds could be shifted within the system easily to cover other needs more adequately.

Whether a claim is major or minor, as long as it is valid and qualified, the Universal Insurance Program would be there to compensate according to priority needs.

The UIP could provide for supplementary income and health care maintenance for seniors and the disabled, and would take the place of all dependency on Medicare and Medicaid payments that have traditionally required a lot of red tape in order to prove everyone is qualified for the help they need at the time it is needed.

With the Universal Insurance Program supported by ShareFlow in operation, all types of inefficient coverage, lack of funds and the tendency to hold back coverage by by existing companies due to useless technicalities would necessarily end and become totally obsolete.

UIP could provide opportunities for countless millions at any age to find their true calling with the help of short term financial aid giving them time to find more optimum employment without undue stress.

The Universal Insurance Program would be poised to fund all reasonable disaster claims submitted by reason of hurricanes, tornadoes, earthquakes, fires, and agriculturally dependent income on flood and drought stricken areas.

Because ShareFlow money could help spearhead a new age of cooperation and caring for everyone, many of the traditional calamities threatening the quality of life for many would be eliminated or reduced.

Especially targeted would be the problems brought on as a result of humanity's previous ignorance that could all be phased out in ways that help improve the system once the qualities of cooperation and trust prove themselves worthy as the basis for a successful operation.

Let us consider a number of examples that span some of the spectrum of insurance claims to get a better idea of how money would be dispensed to recipients from ShareFlow and how the funds would be applied to accomplish the desired coverage.

At the low-value end of the spectrum we have loss or damage to products considered of relatively trivial value such as loss, damage or theft of groceries or personal items that can all be replaced easily without putting in a claim.

In this case, any store where the products are purchased would be expected to take a compassionate stance and willingly replace the items free of charge without a formal claim, since the store would be a business adequately funded with payments to their business account from ShareFlow.

On the other hand, if a business or charity organization purchases a significant quantity of food or other subsistence products for distribution to the needy and the shipment gets lost, stolen or damaged by weather, a claim to the UIP could result in a quick response from ShareFlow to release funds for use as an immediate replacement.

For an example, let us say that Bob Walton is a musician who has just had his guitar stolen which was valued at about $3,000, but has no conclusive proof of the value and only limited witness testimony of his ownership.

In this case, Bob put in a claim to the UIP, and arranged for a representative to come out and record an interview to help validate the information about the guitar.

The representative submits the recording to a standard panel of three at the UIP who determine that Bob is telling the truth about the guitar value and his ownership.

As a result, UIP honors the claim and shifts funds from ShareFlow's master account to Bob's personal account that also resides in ShareFlow to cover the cost of the loss so that Bob can purchase a suitable replacement.

In another example, the Andersons have just had a hail storm that damaged their roof extensively.

Since they are among a group of others in the same area who had a similar experience, Jim Anderson contacts the local office of Appleton Roofing and fills out a form to have their roof inspected by their agent.

After the inspection, Jim is qualified to join a class action claim to the UIP for funding that will cover roof repairs for the Andersons as well as similar repairs for a number of other homes in the same part of town.

UIP verifies that the claim for homes needing repairs or replacement is justified; therefore adequate funds are shifted from the ShareFlow master account to Appleton's business account within ShareFlow to cover costs for all homes that are included in the class action insurance claim.

With that money, Appleton pays their workers to do the labor and uses other funds from their business account to purchase roofing materials for completion of the repairs.

Like all other businesses, Appleton is not authorized to directly shift funds from their business account to personal accounts other than for wages to their employees because businesses would no longer depend upon profit from their clientele but are funded through their business accounts that already reside within ShareFlow.

With the ShareFlow system, all citizens are on a single payer plan for health and medical insurance to automatically cover all normal and routine health maintenance care.

With routine costs for medical coverage, all patient needs can be covered without requiring forms to be filled out since money from ShareFlow can be issued to every medical facility directly to their business accounts.

Funds are kept secure for the purpose of anticipation of coverage for all citizens and for keeping the whole operation of health and medical costs efficiently managed.

For non-urgent major (and perhaps unanticipated) needs for payments not normally covered by traditional insurance companies, claimants would fill out a simple form to submit to the UIP for review to make sure the medical procedures called for are qualified as necessary and justified.

In this case, approved funds would be submitted to the patient by a simple shifting of funds to the patient's personal account within ShareFlow including a notice of approval sent out so that the patient would be aware of the coverage.

Although medical insurance funding for most qualified needs would be virtually automatic, the actual timeline of procedure (operations, exams, etc.) may be subject to a wait time whenever local facilities lack necessary manpower to handle all qualified patients at once.

9 Comprehensive Insurance

If a lack of service personnel or equipment becomes a chronic problem, the UIP would be notified so that money from ShareFlow could be allocated for training of additional qualified workers to meet the increased demand and help balance the system to add more doctors, nurses, technicians and equipment as needed.

All prescription drug coverage could be automatically covered by the UIP as long as monthly premiums paid back into ShareFlow are adjusted equitably for universal coverage and all drugs are dispensed responsibly and securely.

Other cases of comprehensive insurance covered by the UIP would be theft or loss of items of major value, damage or loss of vehicles, damage to homes and equipment due to weather, fire, floods, earthquakes, civil disturbance and even funeral expenses for cremation and memorial services, etc.

All qualified agriculture related claims would be covered by payments made to the business accounts of farmers and ranchers by shifting funds within ShareFlow to appropriate accounts of the claimants.

In some cases class action payments can be made to appropriate business entities so that all necessary work can be accomplished more efficiently.

As should be done by any payout of insurance coverage, funds would be secured by code and put into business accounts for use only in their intended manner.

The UIP would not allow funds to be diverted from any business account to a personal account except in the payout of wages, salaries or compensation payments to the personal accounts of their employees.

Aid to the victims of major weather disasters could rely on funding that would be pre-planned for allocation from the UIP in advance of these events.

Funds would be paid to companies that could construct and distribute temporary housing such as mobile homes for later delivery to victims losing their homes to any weather disaster or other catastrophic event.

9 Comprehensive Insurance

The whole purpose of the UIP's existence would be to make insurance coverage simple, equitable and fairly paid out for all legitimate claims covering everything deemed logical by using one of several ways to direct the funds.

In one case, direct payment from ShareFlow would be paid to the claimant's personal account for use to pay a business entity to do the work of restoring loss or damage.

A different method of payment would ensue whenever there is a large scale coverage needed for anticipated claims coming from many at the same time.

In that case, funds from the UIP would simply shift into business accounts already held in ShareFlow such as with health and medical care providers for example.

In the case of health and medical insurance, payback would be simple and convenient via single payer premiums set adequately and paid to the UIP to help cover costs for anyone else in the plan that would need similar coverage.

~10~
Transaction Values

The next subdivision of SANE I want to refer to is the Universal Transaction Value Program to be set up for the purpose of establishing and keeping in balance the agreed upon standards for wages and prices in a global economy.

It can apply universally and still be flexible enough to adjust for fine tuning with respect to changing conditions such as employment descriptions, environmental changes, variance of products, distribution costs and availability of resources in a fair and equitable manner.

A primary function of the UTVP would be to assign suitable fair and equitable values to all goods and services to hold to the philosophy of value given for value earned or received in all monetary transactions.

The UTVP would also have responsibilities to set fair wages and salaries for every useful work and employment designation throughout the global economy according to the philosophy of value given for value earned.

To work successfully and assure that SANE principles of economics are maintained, the UTVP would need to use flexible designations in a manner that considers real cost differences according to location and cost reductions due to technological advances that occur over time.

It would need to be designed for maximum flexibility according to an evolving economy that is always changing and affecting many variables such as changes in the stress conditions of job duties or changes in available resources or manpower that can drive the costs of any product or service up or down over time.

10 Transaction Values

This program would stipulate that all wages, prices and salaries could no longer be strictly determined by business managers, but would be initially set according to a baseline of payments given for value earned or received.

All wage and salary baselines could be set according to what the average worker is valued at for each designation of employment, enabling managers to tweak rates for the workers within small windows of performance variability.

The scenarios are endless, but taking just one example, consider a case where Lisa of Hispanic descent and Gary of Caucasian background have graduated from the same college with similar degrees in computer science.

It turns out that both are qualified for employment via several job openings at the Meadow Ridge Wind and Solar Energy Corporation in Meadow Ridge.

Both apply at this location for the same type of work as computer programmers where fortunately there is more than one position open for immediate hiring.

Both are hired, and both are assigned equal salary, and since the SANE economy now sets all wages on standards according to job title, there would be no time clocks to keep track of strict working hours.

Both Lisa and Gary earn exactly the same wages with a standard salary rate as long as both perform their duties at least as expected, defined and documented.

Both stay employed at the same type of work, however when either Lisa, Gary or both continue to improve their skills and value according to how well they contribute to the common good, their salary would increase accordingly.

After two years, Lisa decides to move to Sun Valley where the satellite company of Meadow Ridge is located and offers the same employment position at a 10% higher rate due to adjustments in the cost of living.

Since Lisa is a valued employee and has gained skills and experience while at Meadow Ridge, she is awarded an additional rate hike of 10% at Sun Valley.

She is justified for the wage increase totaling 20% without contention by anyone in the corporate offices at Meadow Ridge since the UTVP is notified of her change in venue and has full control of the rates all workers earn.

Meanwhile, Gary has also earned an additional 8% in his salary due to his experience and work performance and remains happily on the job at Meadow Ridge.

He and Lisa stay in contact, and both express their equal satisfaction to be employed by the same company having the same employment description at different locations, even though Lisa at Sun Valley is earning a net 12% higher rate salary over Gary at Meadow Ridge as a result of the rate changes just described.

Even as UTVP operates in a manner to justify wages and prices for all goods and services, it would always do so by essentially allowing only legitimate transfers of money into and out of ShareFlow and would disallow or reduce any other transfers of money that would compromise the purpose of the system.

As a result, such resources previously held in great value such as gold, silver, precious gems, or other physical items traditionally thought of as having significant worth are disallowed to corrupt the free flow of money within the SANE system that UTVP keeps in virtual balance.

Another way to say it is that the UTVP would have to be set up in such a way as to disallow any other medium of traditional value for conversion to official cyber-currency.

Example: If you own a lot of gold, diamonds or other precious commodity, these mediums could not be used for conversion in ShareFlow to gain unearned personal net worth and unbalance the intent of the SANE economy.

With the SANE economy in operation, these former commodities would have value only for the construction of products of specific design and content such as jewelry, which can then be purchased through normal transactions using ShareFlow money already earned.

10 Transaction Values

Once determined, the value standards for products, services and earnings for useful work performed would remain relatively stabilized except for small adjustments due to production and distribution cost changes or other circumstances affecting the perceived value.

Over time, the value of any product or service might be subject to change due to variance of availability and demand, thus the UTVP would act accordingly to make the necessary value changes as convenient as possible.

Likewise, for disbursement of wages, salaries and other payments for work performed, all employment would be classified in standard categories of value for the common good as the general rule.

All set standards would be relatively independent of location, nation or culture and be based upon the type of work involved as well as designated value to society when the work is accomplished.

With the UTVP, any customer would expect to pay about the same cost for any product or service anywhere, since independence of location could encourage the goal of mutual cooperation and trust in a global economy.

Any work performed that accomplishes essentially the same result would be rewarded approximately the same wage, salary or direct payment independent of location, gender, age, culture or other factors that are not relevant for consideration in judging output and quality of work.

Another idea would be to calculate the averages of all manufacturing costs and their costs of distribution at all locations so that all employees could work for a standard wage with respect to their given job description.

Even with that there might be necessary adjustments allowed if deemed logical to make the system work better.

For this effort to work successfully, the UTVP would need to determine expenses of production and distribution that are normally location dependent and set actual costs according to a global average to factor out as many cost differentials for workers of different nations, cultures and locations as possible.

Production and distribution costs that would normally be different in certain locations could be averaged instead of having cost differentials applied to the consumer.

Shopping for value at other locations based upon price consideration alone would be outmoded since every item whether it be groceries, pharmaceuticals, appliances, autos, fuel purchases, airline tickets, etc. would cost virtually the same independent of where the item is purchased.

In a similar manner, services rendered would all cost about the same independent of location so that useless time, energy and travel expenses trying to shop for best value would be outmoded.

The only comparison shopping of products or services should depend on factors other than price, such as quality of products or the quality of services rendered.

Comparison shopping in any given location could still use typical capitalistic principles of competition to ensure high product quality control, but would not need to offer bargains at lower cost.

Instead, all businesses would do better to compete for customer satisfaction involving the quality of products and how the sales personnel deal with their customers.

With the UTVP in operation, there would no longer be an incentive for management to try to force employees to work overtime without pay since businesses would no longer rely on profit to stay in business.

All work responsibilities could be defined in terms of standard duty definitions and thus any overtime would be compensated fairly and adequately.

In this respect, no employees would feel abused for doing hard work on a volunteer basis.

Store coupons would no longer be necessary because all products would have a relatively fixed cost and would no longer need coupons or other incentives for customers to buy the products at a lower price.

This makes the UTVP an important subdivision of the SANE economy since it increases overall efficiency and eliminates wasted time, effort and money traditionally used to advertise and goad the average consumer into buying more than they want and stuff they don't always need on the incentive of paying lower prices.

This means that constructive 'capitalism' would not be dead so that competition in the market place could still occur, but would no longer be based upon the focus of profit and stress over reducing costs.

It would simply be in the form of advertising for the sole purpose of emphasizing the quality of products and services offered to potential customers of any business.

All transaction values would be maintained by the UTVP subsystem of the SANE economic structure using ShareFlow to manage all funds for payment of products or services, or for wages and salaries given out on the basis of value received for value earned.

~11~
Employment Matching

For the SANE economy to be considered optimally efficient, one of the logical subsystems for inclusion could be an all-inclusive matching service for job opportunities to match suitable employers with job seekers in a universal employment matching program called the (UEMP).

It could and should be global in scope so that suitable matchups with available job openings of any description for any and all applicants seeking employment regardless of location can be found to optimize work situations.

The UEMP would be part of the network of SANE economics available online throughout the world in order to cover all employment opportunities currently available to any qualified applicant, classification and work interest.

The main purpose of UEMP would be to match job opportunities with the most appropriate job seekers who are looking for their best choice of employment in terms of description, location, salary and benefits.

It would consider special interests, work experience, skills, education and other factors that would be important for employers and applicants to base their decisions upon.

The main advantage of the UEMP would be to open up a massive number of new employment opportunities at all skill and labor descriptions that qualify for work related to the general welfare and common good of everyone.

Using UEMP, all factors for best matchups would be systematically identified for general consideration because there would always be funds available from ShareFlow to pay for many new openings not dependent upon the profit motive in a standard money-driven environment.

11 Employment Matching

With all SANE economic subsystems in operation, the motivation of trying to always keep corporate profits at a maximum is nullified, thereby taking away one of the main reason why opportunities and benefits to employees and job openings are held to an illogical and unfair minimum.

Being global and covering all employment openings available anywhere in the world, the complete pool of all job opportunities in any and every country can be easily compared for best possible matchups.

Due to sheer numbers of comparisons worldwide, it is quite clear that most any job seeker is likely to be matched up with many employment opportunities to choose from at any given moment in real time.

Information available to each job seeker could include management preferences, numbers of applicants already applying for each opening, the education and experience desired but not necessarily required, and anything else they should know to make it easy for every job seeker to apply for any job opening in the master data base.

The online information for every opening presented by the UEMP could be continuously updated in real time by having each company update their current information in the data base as new openings become available.

To be fair to all job seekers, each company could offer incentives to encourage each applicant to consider over all benefits of what their management can provide if they are hired as a new employee.

Matching job seekers with job openings should be a two-way street and be well-balanced to match the needs of both the new employees as well as the management.

With SANE economics in operation globally, each job description for new employees would no longer have to be slanted to satisfy only the management requirements.

Indeed UEMP job descriptions could include all the variables that any new job seeker is interested in such as salaries, vacation and sick time, educational opportunities, ambiance and variability of job locations, adjustable work hours, on-the job training, contributory value of openings to society, available housing, travel costs for relocation and any other pertinent information regarding opportunities and benefits that are likely to open up in the near future.

The goal of UEMP should be to find employment for any job seeker in as short a time as possible, and thus keep everyone who is willing and able to find their best choice within all available openings as determined by a match comparison of skills, talents and personality.

Employment matching would be a network function linking the other subsystems of SANE to operate most efficiently in performing a job matching opportunity for everyone seeking a new job or a different profession.

It could work well for anyone regardless of previous experience, status in life, gender, race, ethnic background, age or any factor considered important to a person's ability to perform job description requirements.

UEMP would provide continuous opportunities for all employers to fill needed positions if and when they arise.

Most importantly it would be needed for job seekers to find the right kind of work to enable compatibility and long term satisfaction in whatever type of profession they are looking for, and are qualified to be accepted into.

The matching process would be designed and operated in such a manner to assure that there would always be more job openings available than job seekers.

This condition would help insure confidence, trust and cooperation between job seekers and employers and help assure that the most desirable openings are filled first.

At the same time this is taking place, UEMP should operate in such a way as to phase out the unnecessary and low-priority jobs in favor of employment more beneficial to the health and well-being of society in general.

UEMP would exist to aid in the effort of bringing the global unemployment rate to near zero and maintain that rate so that no job seeker would have to spend excessive time or stress in seeking placement they believe they are most interested in and qualified for.

By mutually satisfying job seekers and the management of the companies they work for, it is a win-win situation and a benefit to society as a whole since happy employees are usually the most productive, dependable and beneficial in their work contributions to the economy at all levels.

For anyone currently employed and thinking about a change, UEMP would likely act as a guide to something better suited to their talents, their personality, their skills and their interests.

For some it could open up new horizons they would never have considered if they were still saddled in a work situation having money concerns as their main priority.

In some cases it could open up awareness of a wide field of new opportunities and possibly a whole new career direction, including specific opportunities of stepping into a field of development they never previously thought they could actually qualify for.

Whenever positions of employment are phased out, UEMP would be able to offer all previous employees new opportunities for the same or similar type of work close to their same location, or point the direction to an alternate idea that could prove even more resonant with their basic education, skills and interests.

And just like each of the other subdivisions of SANE working together in an efficient and user-friendly manner, the UEMP could contribute to the vitally important part of helping build motivation and enthusiasm in people of all levels of education, experience, skills and capabilities no matter what their station in life might be.

UEMP could provide optimum opportunities to find just the right employment for any job seeker to improve the quality of life for themselves and their families while contributing to society in a way that would provide greater professionalism and better work ethics resulting from the evolution in technology that provides better products with less effort and not dependent on the profit motive.

Having the right fit for employment at any level helps generate one's personal pride and accomplishment by way of work performance of high contributory value.

It gives an added benefit to the economy reinforcing what I call a self-construct mechanism that helps to phase out the money-driven system of slavery to money that has held all of us in a tight grip for far too long.

Having optimum matching of employment with job seekers would undoubtedly benefit social interaction since there would be more time freed up for all the non-work related aspects of life.

People of all nations and cultures have a much greater sense of freedom when they are not constantly worried about how to pay the bills for earning a living in less than optimum conditions, or having to endure mismatches of employment interests just to earn money to live on.

When people are in a good place with their personal finances, they have more time for their social life by being able to interact more freely with friends and family.

This creates a beneficial set of dynamics continuously working to benefit the quality of life for many at all levels of the social spectrum in different but related ways.

The UEMP matching process would document each job description, duties, benefits, compensation and other necessary details in real time, and store them in various profile documentaries accessible at all local UEMP offices to compare with profiles submitted by applicants.

Job seekers for any professional description would fill out a comprehensive profile in order to have it submitted into the master profile database for comparison with every job profile submitted by employers seeking new hires.

The UEMP database would be periodically updated as new profile information comes through in real time.

11 Employment Matching

Once all information submitted by current job seekers is compared with the database description of available job openings, compatibility matching scores between 90% and 100 % might be considered as the window of acceptability for applicant notification that they should research all the openings with those scores as worthy of consideration.

Each job seeker would get all their online notifications indicating job openings that show a mutual compatibility score of at least 90% for them to select from and consider for further communication and interviews.

Let's look at a few examples of how the UEMP would work under a ShareFlow funding environment to insure an efficient operation that identifies the attributes of mutual compatibility in employment matching for a global master database operation.

The following examples are meant to illustrate how UEMP could work fairly and equitably for any business, corporation, or government offering employment, as well as for job seekers who are seeking employment suited to their qualifications and interests.

Donald Wilson lives in a small town in Missouri and just completed his degrees in mathematics and computer applications and is now ready to apply to UEMP for his career goal as a scientific programmer.

He fills out a comprehensive form he accessed online that details his education, work experience and life style that is pertinent to his desired field of employment.

The profile takes in many items of interest to future employers regarding his education, experience, interests, personality traits, family responsibilities and desired salary level as well as preferred locations for hire.

When Donald gets the readout of current matchups, he finds that there are a total of 18 openings with mutual compatibility matchup ratings from 90.7 % to 96.3%.

97

11 Employment Matching

These job openings are currently located in various cities around the world, several of which are situated in cities and towns within 750 miles of his home town.

It turns out that there are three companies of special interest because of their locations and reputations of being highly favored by their existing employees.

Donald arranges a time for a personal interview with management from each company who then schedule their two-way conversations to occur at his home computer.

After these interviews are completed, Donald gets employment offers from two of the three companies to visit their locations for subsequent hiring information.

After careful consideration and further interviews, he accepts the job opening located in Colorado because the type of location he prefers is in a community that offers majestic mountains as a backdrop to both his place of employment and his presumed residence.

Now consider Amy Dawson working as a waitress for many years living in a large city in the Midwest.

In her spare time she has earned a degree in veterinary medicine to qualify her as a veterinary assistant.

Amy fills out a profile for UEMP that details her past work history, education, lifestyle, personality traits, and other pertinent details that are of interest to professionals in her chosen career field.

When Amy gets her readout of current matchups for veterinary medicine, she finds a total of 27 openings with mutual compatibility ratings of 91.9 % to 98.5% currently available including several within 200 miles from home.

Amy decides to attend interviews with four different veterinary hospitals using the online video method in two-way appearances and conversations.

Once the interviews are completed, she decides to wait a few weeks to see which offices will present her with job offers because all four facilities are given high marks with respect to employee satisfaction, management style, salary and ambiance in a quiet small town environment.

Two job offers come through for her, so after a series of additional interviews with paid travel expenses to both locations, she decides to accept one of them on the basis of two considerations.

The offer she chooses is located in the town where she has relatives who live close by and have encouraged her to relocate to an affordable apartment complex near a natural wooded area with a quiet stream running close by.

The other consideration is that the particular vet office she has chosen has a higher rating of employee satisfaction with the management style that Amy indicated as a priority compared to the other facility having similar attractions and even a 12% higher starting salary.

James Lacey is 37, is married with two children and living in Kalamazoo, MI where he has been employed as an auto mechanic for all of his professional life.

Recently however, he started thinking about changing professions, so he took an online aptitude test measuring several levels of IQ, interests and skills in a variety of fields of endeavor to help him decide what might be a good alternative to being an auto repairman.

The results indicated that he should apply for a job in the renewable clean energy field that might include solar, wind and other forms of renewable clean energy having openings accessible through a matching profile on UEMP.

When filling out his profile form online, his interest perked up in response to wind energy technologies being advertised and available for consideration at companies throughout the U.S. and other countries in South America, Europe, Asia and Africa.

When Jim received his results for potential matchups, he was a bit overwhelmed that so many renewable energy opportunities now existed all over the global environment.

11 Employment Matching

For wind energy alone there were 108 matches for his interests, skills and mechanical abilities, with a total of 15 within the U.S. and the rest all over the world.

After receiving the results, he decided to submit a revised profile that focused more on his specific interest in wind energy companies specializing in the production of vertical axis wind rotors (a favorite topic for conversation).

Many were working with the mechanics of putting together the various sized units compatible for individual home use such as some highly efficient rotors that operate well in low to medium wind conditions and are mounted conveniently on roof tops or poles.

Upon receipt of the revised profile match results, Jim was able to focus on selecting from the total number of matchups which now numbered 26 in various locations throughout the world and included 11 within the U.S.

But this time Jim noted that one of the companies he had matched with was located in Denmark with a rating of 97.4% mutual compatibility.

Scandinavia was an area of the world Jim had dreamed about seeing one day, so after researching the credentials of the company called Gentle Vortex located in Aarhus, he decided he would make that the No.1 priority to accept if offered employment.

Subsequent communications with the company reps netted a job offer at 15% higher salary than he asked for.

After conferring with his wife Dana and their children who all supported the idea, he and his family moved to Denmark where he is now enthusiastically helping to put together the various components of wind rotor generators necessary to complete many renewable clean wind energy conversion units suitable for individual home use.

The vertical rotor units that Jim now works with are applicable for countless homes in the nation of Denmark and other areas in northern Europe.

11 Employment Matching

As a result not only did Jim and his family get to live in one of their dream locations in Europe, but his business trips now take him and his family back to the States for an occasional visit, and to other Scandinavian countries as a consultant in wind energy technology.

To handle employment and applicant matching ideally for all available positions of employment, there should be redundant accessibility to the master database at every city, town and locality where UEMP has an office.

Every office should include non-local employment and applicant processing to provide a truly universal method for matching open jobs with a complete pool of applicants wherever the openings and applicants are located.

It is no secret that a universal employment matching process would be quite an enormous undertaking, yet if money was no longer the limitation, but freely flowing through a global ShareFlow cyber-currency transaction system, any developers of the matching process would no longer have to worry about excessive developmental costs.

This author believes that this effort is another idea whose time has surely come to pass.

~12~
Capital Allocations

I envision another subsystem of SANE I refer to as a Universal Capital Allocation Program (UCAP) set up to allocate sufficient funding for research and development of new enterprises, and provide necessary support to any existing business for responsible expanded operations.

UCAP would be in operation to allocate and distribute proper funding directly out of ShareFlow to entrepreneurs who need help for developing a worthy enterprise.

Potential entrepreneurs would need to present a valid case for ensuring that the new enterprise or changes to an existing one will result in improvements in technology and quality of life applicable to the common good.

Any new invention, product, service or expansion of an existing business always needs some capital to initiate, and may require additional funding to be in proper balance with supply and demand.

An obvious responsibility of UCAP would be to determine which entrepreneurial efforts should qualify for allocated funds, and which do not meet basic standards unless proper modifications are documented.

UCAP would allocate funding to individuals for any qualified enterprise resulting from entrepreneurial efforts, or become available for expansion of existing businesses, schools, corporations, agricultural pursuits, training and other functions needing financial backing for increasing capacity or quality of products offered.

UCAP would be responsible for maintaining sustained funding for improving education at all levels from K-12 on up, and be the prime driver for support of all priorities in public education including math, science, engineering and social interaction curriculum.

I see a prioritized need for social interaction classes for training in research and development of programs to help develop and maintain emotional and mental health in our youth, and provide freedom from drug and alcohol abuse for everyone at any age.

Important social interaction classes could be funded to teach young people the necessary skills to live in harmony and cooperation with their peers in forming healthy social relationships and mature interactions with every level of society at home and abroad regardless of race, culture, age differences, religion or ethnic background.

For entrepreneurship, the UCAP would be set up to determine which projects are feasible for beginning a new venture and which projects can qualify for expansion.

There are hundreds of entrepreneurial efforts created for bringing more renewable clean energy technologies to the forefront of public awareness; but to date most have been suppressed by ignorance involving money concerns of the controllers, foremost of which are Big Oil, Big Coal and even those insisting that nuclear energy is the answer.

At the time of this writing there is a great need for adequate funding of renewable clean energy technologies deemed of highest priority, but also a clear mandate for legal enforcement of laws to guarantee non-interference by the fierce opposition of money-driven interests.

The UCAP would provide necessary funding for the most promising cutting-edge renewable and clean energy technologies to date that need to go full speed-ahead.

It would give financial assistance to provide efficient mass production of a vast number of products to satisfy anticipated high demands from the majority of citizens who wish to break away from fossil fuel dependencies.

Obvious examples needing adequate financial support are the entrepreneurships that work with ongoing research and development of various conversions of solar and wind energy to electricity for use in a variety of energy needs.

Simply installing solar paneling on the roofs of homes for producing electricity off the grid has become the main innovation for producing renewable clean energy and can be an excellent resource for locations anywhere south of the Arctic Circle or north of the Antarctic Circle.

There are many promising technologies involving solar and wind energy that can be set up over vast land areas around the world where either resource or both working together can deliver convenient year-around supplies of renewable clean energy for heating, cooling and the means for storing electricity in high tech battery units.

Working together with a variety of new technologies now being developed, they show promise of easily phasing out the fossil fuel industries forever, and certainly for the good of the environment and the well-being of all future generations hoping for a better world.

With the UCAP in operation, the funding of all solar energy projects would be a straight forward procedure by simply allocating funds automatically from ShareFlow as long as each project is documented as being sufficiently viable, necessary and a benefit to society in general.

In conjunction with the many solar energy projects undergoing research and development are the technologies involving wind energy turbines and wind energy support equipment to allow homeowners to install localized energy conversion systems that can be either wholly or partially energy independent.

Since wind energy exists in varying but mostly useful proportions at about every location on earth, it would be a no-brainer to take advantage of a viable mass production effort of wind turbines, generators and storage devices for production of renewable clean wind energy.

These conversion units would provide electrical energy sources independent of electrical company network grids, and be supported directly by money from ShareFlow and managed through UCAP.

Perhaps the ultimate source of energy available at any point in time and space in our visible Universe is not yet well advertised, but viably referred to as zero point.

Zero point energy is the latent, invisible (and ordinarily undetectable) ambient energy left after all other sources of energy are removed from any region of space existing at a temperature of absolute zero.

This latent energy is effectively an infinite source of ultra-high frequency wave energy that holds a potential of being able to efficiently convert to electricity for everyday use in homes, businesses or powering of vehicles on land, sea or air, or outer space to power spacecraft.

Many believe that this latent energy at any point in space (outer space or otherwise) will be the wave of the future to replace everything else including solar, wind and all other sources of energy (clean or otherwise).

There is credible evidence that zero point technology for conversion to usable electricity has been notoriously suppressed by the money controllers, notably the fossil fuel industries with Big Oil leading the assault.

Hundreds of efforts over the last century including Nikola Tesla's experiments beginning in the late 1800's and to this date still go wanting for support because all would-be entrepreneurs have had their patents suppressed, bought out, or threatened with personal injury or threats to family members unless they abandoned their efforts.

In order to correct this situation, at least two things need to take place:

1. Adequate laws have to be developed to insure and protect any would-be entrepreneurs from suppression or harassment so that no matter who is seeking support for a clean energy project, he or she can find out if they qualify without outside interference.

2. A reliable source of funding needs to be available to allocate start-up funds in such a manner as to give every entrepreneur working for clean energy sources a clear path to accomplish their goal.

The UCAP would have the responsibility to determine which projects are viable for qualification and worthy of funding from ShareFlow.

As an illustration of how UCAP would allocate funds to an entrepreneur in the clean energy field, let's use an example of how a likely project that may already have been developed would be approved.

Howard Anderson has been a talented employee of a company called Gentle Vortex which produces wind rotor generators of various design for general use on homes and businesses using efficient conversion to store electricity.

Having a keen interest in zero point energy, Howard spends several years doing intensive research on projects that have already proven themselves successful on a small scale to run motors for demonstration purposes.

Howard believes he has a logical means to extract just enough ZPE energy to transform certain frequencies for a continuous 24/7 operation in charging batteries to power motors including their use in cars, other vehicles and other means of application using electricity off the grid.

Howard puts in a well planned formal request to the UCAP for funds to hire several others to begin a new business developing what he calls the Ultimate Battery Charger that would operate by extracting energy directly from the zero point energy resource.

After careful review of Howard's plan, the panel at UCAP that approves or disapproves of applications sends the plan back for added information to clarify his claim of continuous and efficient operation.

Howard does some more research, and after a small modification resubmits the proposal with his clarification.

12 Capital Allocations

After a short waiting period, he hears that his request has been approved for funding over a five year contractual agreement with instructions for submitting updates on a timely basis to verify progress.

Within two years, Howard and Associates perfect the technology and are soon operating the business trying to keep up with a barrage of orders from all over the U.S and other countries to purchase the Ultimate Battery Charger.

Aside from renewable clean energy technologies, there are always new inventions, products and services that need funding whether they appear to be of global adaptation or just something of local interest only.

UCAP would assure that potentially wasted money and efforts are minimized and that all monetary support requests are handled on a priority timeline.

The rule would be that as long as a new invention, innovation, discovery or expansion of an existing business can be validated as beneficial to society and contributes to the common good in an efficient and credible fashion, it would be given the necessary funding through allocations for release from ShareFlow as determined by UCAP.

~13~
Renewable Clean Energy

The question here is simply 'How would renewable clean energy development help our global society rid itself of the entrapment of a money-driven world?

Indeed, how can we archive the demands of monetary accountability, money manipulation, balanced accounts, loans, credit and debt that have become so acceptable that acquisition of money seems to be our primary goal in life?

Would having a world completely free of dependency on fossil fuels be a major player in freeing us all from the need for pursuing money, profit, credit and debt?

It seems that as long as oil drilling, the rest of the fossil fuel industries and the business related interests continue unabated in their relentless imposition on the environment, there may be little or no visible progress in establishing a moneyfree way of doing business.

The reasons for this quagmire and the descriptions of all the detrimental effects to the planet are too numerous to list here of course, but can be touched upon briefly.

So let's take a look at how a clean energy environment could trigger an unstoppable move away from our money-dependent entrenchment to a moneyfree future for us all.

Let us visualize a methodology of running an efficient global economy that includes some prioritized methods of developing renewable clean energy resources to completely replace the use of fossil fuels and nuclear power plants

It is also reasonable to note that renewable clean energy could make the production and distribution of products and services more efficient and cost effective by mass producing the infrastructure required to support operations.

13 Renewable Clean Energy

Using clean energy technology also has a beneficial side effect of taking the focus off the acquisition of money and putting it into establishing true quality of life for all.

Most technologies for renewable clean energy have been known for many generations, but have yet to be considered top priority with the average citizen except in a few small countries such as Iceland, Germany and the Netherlands just to name a few.

There is a growing interest in some countries that are beginning to see the need to adapt to Climate Change and are becoming aware of the role that the EPA and other organizations are playing in trying to establish and maintain a healthy global environment.

Unfortunately these sensible priorities have not been taken seriously enough for the leaders and legislators calling the shots and making the laws to realize they are responsible to help develop an international working cooperative.

At the time of this writing, most have not learned the simple truth that it is their responsibility to take charge and allow adequate planning and financial support to take the leap from focusing on profit and debt concerns to thinking more about sustainable ways of living to enable the general population of every nation to have a healthy life style.

Woefully illustrated are the environmental standards that keep nations still grounded in fossil fuel dependence and suppressed from supporting entrepreneurs who demonstrate a much better way to do business.

For many localities within the two largest contributors of air, water and ground pollution, namely the United States and China, the cost of cleaning up the sources of pollution and responding to the medical expenses in virtually all the health field industries are now of utmost concern.

In a moneyfree world, this would never be a problem.

The entrapment of a profit-driven world has made the priority of staying healthy out of reach for vast numbers and segments of the world population.

Solutions to this enigma are well-known of course, but the implementation of the solution has been suppressed for the most part due to the profit motive obsession being the unavoidable result of humanity's choices on how they set up their priorities and how they select their leaders to run the government and control their economy.

The mindset of claiming that this is the way 'things are done' is abundantly true, but at the same time abundantly clear that the easy money motive is always the trump card when change is logically suggested.

Fortunately, the proposed ECU Network (explained in later chapters) that leads to a completely money-free system becomes a natural dynamic when the fossil fuel industries will finally be stopped and be forced to quit and go home.

Change will happen when the fossil fuel industries recognize that a complete transition to renewable clean energies would actually be more profitable and benefit not only themselves and the masses of every nation, but also the rest of the top money dogs in ways none of them have previously wanted to admit.

As long as the big money racket remains adhered to the profit motive that results in the acquisition of unlimited quantities of money, power and control over many others in a hostile environment, nothing will change very soon.

It is clear to many with just average intelligence and the awareness of current affairs in the world that the money-driven society we live in inevitably leaves all the players including some of the controllers themselves wondering how the economy got trapped in a perpetual state of slavery to a system that has outgrown its usefulness.

It is also quite clear that nothing to change the system can happen soon until the profit motive fixations of the money driven system are driven out of the public mindset.

In the minds of progressives everywhere, nowhere has the idea that 'money is the root of all evil' been more clearly illustrated than in the antics of the fossil fuel industry.

13 Renewable Clean Energy

Clearly the powers that be have been given the choice of phasing out oil and gas drilling and coal mining in favor of sustainable choices of renewable clean energy.

The long term benefits of such a choice are enormous, but so far the choice for aggressive development of a variety of clean energy alternatives has mostly fallen on deaf ears.

Obviously the CEOs of these corporations have taken the low road in favor of easy short term financial benefit of entrenched profiteering that bloats their financial base at the expense of the global environment.

By doing so, they ignore the health of the masses and ignore the responsibility of recognizing the much greater value of having safe and healthy clean energy innovations available to replace fossil fuel dependency.

There is much good news however, although it seems unnecessarily slow in becoming apparent to the masses who need reassurance that all is not lost.

The changes are beginning to make themselves known in a slow but inevitable phase out of coal along with some effort in limiting oil and gas drilling by raising concerns over the fracking methods that affect ground water which harms the immediate localities near the drilling operations.

There seems to be a slow recognition that even the profit motive can still exist alive and well with energy alternatives; but is beginning to raise the question of how important are immediate wealth and profit motivations when compared to rational alternatives in clean energy that work for creating a sustainable future that benefits everyone.

Clean energy technologies have been slowly picking up steam (pun intended) over several generations of new age thinking even as the implementation of systems to replace fossil fuel usage develops on many fronts.

Excruciatingly slow and politically vulnerable are the cogs turning in the wheels of progress that churn out only small successes over time, but are seen in the form of visible installations of affordable solar and wind energy systems.

13 Renewable Clean Energy

Even though many progressives find it easy to see the long term benefits of a completely renewable clean energy future, they recognize that to get to that place may take a long time, unusual effort and a monumental change in the way humanity thinks about money and its purpose.

To phase into renewable clean energy alternatives and out of the unrealistic fossil fuel dependency that has plagued the planet for centuries is considered a monumental effort due to unrelenting resistance of Big Oil and Big Money.

Even so it would be like the adage of saying 'one small step for man, and one giant step for mankind', because the ramifications of taking the profit motives away from the big oil, gas and coal executives would undoubtedly open the door to more and better jobs, and a more sustainable future for the entire global economy.

This is why aggressive steps for renewable clean energy technologies are a vital step along the way to establishing an 'out with the old money-driven system' and 'in with the new moneyfree reality for our future' which will hopefully occur soon and possibly during the next generation.

A moneyfree way of doing business will undoubtedly become a reality for the planet at some point along the way, so it is important to understand the feasibility of taking small steps now, including the visualization of how each step can bring about significant change sooner than we can imagine.

Once a real SANE economy or something close to it becomes a reality, a major step will have been accomplished to remove the detrimental effect of money limitations that have so far prevented the entire global environment from developing renewable clean energy as the standard in lieu of fossil fuel dependency.

At the time of this writing, the choices for renewable clean energy are basically three different technologies, but all can work either separately or together to be supportive of air, water and ground cleanup from all venues of pollution that threatens the health of every world citizen including the so-called wealthy-elite.

Fortunately two of these sources (solar and wind energy conversion systems) are gaining momentum and presenting an inevitable push against the fossil fuel industry in a variety of ways that continue to improve in technological efficiency.

In many ways, that reality makes the whole concept of renewable clean energy not only a palatable choice for those still concerned about cost, but easily demonstrable to be far superior to fossil fuel usage in other ways too numerous and significant to mention in this writing.

As long as a catastrophic global disaster (nuclear war or a large asteroid strike for example) does not demolish our civilization along with it the infrastructure of clean energy technologies that have already been developed, the skilled and educated work force and the will of the nations' leaders to accept clean energy change will become inevitable.

The removal of money concerns as the limiting factor of consideration will likely bring in a deluge of orders for many clean energy products for home and business usage.

And in the thinking of some scientists and many laymen, there is powerful awareness and support for some of the zero point energy systems being researched for efficiency when they are finally developed and available on the market.

Right now we have options in the form of solar, wind and zero point conversion systems to phase out and end the global dependency on fossil fuels from any source.

It is logical that the global economy can eventually wean itself away from the profit motive and embrace a sensible energy program based upon a workable form of moneyfree operations to keep economics in an efficient balance.

The advantage of these three sources of energy working in an optimum arrangement of two or all three together is that they can each produce electricity for convenient storage as DC or converted to AC current for direct power usage.

13 Renewable Clean Energy

These plus other systems including those that isolate and store hydrogen gas can be sourced at most any location on Earth, and can be produced and distributed in portable units for convenient installation and replacement by way of mass production applied to a variety of standard modular designs.

The effects of switching to an energy policy grounded and based upon the use of renewable clean energies instead of fossil fuels can be far reaching in a SANE based economy where the traditional limitations of lack of money would no longer be applicable in most cases.

Consider the effect of an economy depending only on the use of renewable clean energy for agriculture, medical facilities and social infrastructure, where everything depends upon labor, the job market, and the balance between supply and demand for goods and services.

With agriculture, the use of clean energy and the auto-release of funds from ShareFlow would likely result in a major shift away from extensive farming to intensive use of greenhouse growing for creating healthier food with greater efficiency to feed the planet.

When the mindset of conservatism limiting the release of adequate money is finally pushed aside in favor of policies that benefit the common good, the sky's the limit in what kind of domino effect that can roll through every avenue of commerce, industry and the realization that we are no longer divided, but finally united in a common goal.

Essentially ShareFlow could always respond to the need for additional funding to enable farmers and ranchers to choose locally intensive operations such as greenhouses for responding to a potentially larger demand for fresh produce and a correspondingly smaller demand for meat that could all be produced efficiently on small farms and ranches.

For commerce in general, the SANE economy and the related shift to renewable clean energy could certainly have a sizeable effect on the direction of future technologies.

13 Renewable Clean Energy

Living a simpler life closer to nature's bounty is likely to reduce the demand for extensive increase in technological changes that would normally cost considerable amounts of funding to shift workers for those purposes.

In other words, a shift in priorities of the average citizen could have a profound effect on the total global demand for energy conversion making it even more cost efficient and easier to phase out of fossil fuel usage.

For many generations we have lived in a world of steep demand for energy while attempting to respond to rapid technological growth that is out of balance with true quality of life for the average citizen.

Some of the normal demand in our money-driven world has to do with hauling large loads of construction products over long distances with increased energy needs.

Using renewable clean energies can reduce that demand by encouraging the use of local production centers in small town communities for a large number or products.

This would allow a more efficient operation of general construction and production plants for all goods at local distribution points, all of which would not be a problem in a SANE economy that would allow adequate funds as needed in response to what is required for the common good.

Keeping in mind that the philosophy of moneyfree can work in a step-wise fashion to help us change our thinking in order to eliminate the significance of money; let us take a closer look at how solar, wind, and ultimately zero point energy usage can go a long way to make it happen.

It would make sense to develop the structuring of both solar and wind conversion systems to be designed and used in tandem, not only for maximum efficiency, but logically for esthetic properties that permit the placement of such structures to be less obvious as well as being designed for ambiance that fits well with the general surroundings.

Although many types of structuring can occur for both solar and wind units, for the purpose of this story, I assume a mass production of solar, wind and zero point energy combinations adjusted according to an optimum ratio of use involving all three sources can contribute to overall energy efficiency at any given locality on Earth.

For solar units, I see portable units easily set up that can be placed favorably to take advantage of being directly in line with the sun at noon.

For wind energy conversion, I would recommend the type that uses vertical axis rotation like turbines that catch the wind no matter which direction it is blowing.

I envision a 100% renewable clean energy policy for all homes and businesses within a locality, city or nation, and ultimately the entire global community by simply using a combination of solar, wind and zero point in every case.

Using solar and wind to start with and then replacing some of these units with zero point systems when they are finally approved for funding would be the logical next step.

For starters, each ratio could be defined as the best case combination of modular solar and wind energy conversion units set up in response to a scientifically approved measure of best case solar to wind conditions at each locality.

The number of units of each type would be determined according to how much dependence on solar compared to wind energy should be utilized to create the most efficient optimization for any given locality.

As a ball-park example, considering ratios as a function of latitude alone, the number of clean energy conversion units set up in general would use more solar constructs in lower latitudes and more wind units in the higher latitudes.

When considering location above sea level as a variable, the previous ratio of units for any home or a business could change accordingly, by considering a greater wind-unit ratio at high-wind elevations, and a greater solar- unit ratio at low-wind elevations.

Topography of the land is an important consideration for both urban and rural locations, but obviously each case could be based upon which ratio gives the best results when the sun is not available or when wind is not sufficient for significant contributions.

The good news is that a general reliance on standardized mass production of all modules distributed as a ratio of solar to wind and zero point could always provide a contribution of stored energy, which makes the energy storage easier to match to power company grids using AC current.

Another part of the good news is that the stored DC electrical energy could be put to use to charge batteries for electric cars and other vehicles while they are not in use.

And for a SANE economy being the global standard, the significance of cost would be greatly reduced compared to our present profit-driven way of doing business.

With a SANE economical experience in full operation, renewable clean energy innovations would no longer be limited by financial concerns and would be developed in a way that even the conservatives of the day would have little trouble in cheering about.

Even the conservatives in today's world would cheer if they could say yes to an aggressive development of clean energy along with an assertive phase out of big oil, coal and natural gas knowing that it would benefit them in ways they had never thought could actually occur.

~14~
Monetary Accountability

The concepts of monetary accountability and financial responsibility have been considered the unwritten law of a civilized society for countless generations.

They have focused on the almost universal aversion to allow anyone to obtain any item of significant monetary value without forced accountability to pay a bill.

The purpose of forced accountability is supposed to keep everyone 'honest' and fully responsible to contribute their fair share of satisfying the philosophy of 'value given for value received'.

So with that moral and ethical philosophy firmly in place to get along in this world, what could possibly go wrong?

In fact the idea that everyone must pay their way for everything in life except for giving gifts is so ingrained in human nature that no one questions why anyone should think differently, even if society changes in such a way that that the strict obligation to pay money for everything in life should no longer apply.

Not only has the accountability of money become the root of many forms of litigation that have existed since the dawn of civilization, but it has turned many basically honest folks into 'criminals' whenever they find they cannot pay their bills or get subsistence basics due to lack of funds.

For a simple example, consider a homeless person who for whatever reason is faced with desperation over how to find enough food to live on, realizes he has just discovered an easy way to steal what he needs to survive.

Even though he could have made better choices to solve his problem, his desperation triggers his choice of what to do, so being faced with the opportunity to steal some basic subsistence items, he makes the decision to steal food and is caught and arrested in doing so.

In general, the law does not look kindly at extenuating circumstances, so in his case he is convicted of a crime and put in jail where he suddenly finds that his subsistence needs are met because the law mandates that all prisoners are to be given life essentials no matter what their crime might be.

Something about that very common situation strikes me as being out of synch with common sense and justice...

As a primary source of the problem, it seems to me that our money-driven society has in one way or another been the root cause of his plight in the first place because his life experience may have gone into a downward spiral due to a number of extenuating circumstances.

One of these may have been a stressful employment experience that could have acted as a trigger for a domino effect to create other reasons for being homeless.

Do not take this to mean we should blame everything that goes wrong in life on the system (which I assertively do not), but regardless of the root cause in his case, a question bodes well stating - Just who are the real criminals?

Are we to consider every homeless person who steals food or some other subsistence basics a criminal?

Or do we need to focus our attention more on those who withhold necessary funds to take care of the basics for him and countless other men, women and children going through similar experiences and end up being homeless?

When we talk about 'accountability' in financial matters, it would seem to me that the subject should go both ways by holding everyone accountable, not only to 'pay their bills on time' but also the countless individuals on the other end of the transactions who could have helped prevent poverty by supporting laws to have subsistence basics available to all.

Surely we can apply the word 'accountable' to the ones who already have more than enough money they need for an arbitrarily comfortable life, but because of legalities being on their side, still find it necessary to enforce payment of all bills including those applied to the many who are trying to scrape for their basics due to inadequate income.

Although it is certainly legal to require strict payment of all bills in a 'value payment for value received' manner, the question still bodes well asking: Who are all those morally and ethically responsible for a homeless person's decision to steal subsistence basics?'

Since Congress is given the authority to issue money for responsible social programs including education, why not hold them responsible to allocate enough funding for basic subsistence so that homelessness becomes obsolete?

Why cannot everyone have adequate education to direct their talents into life choices that would likely prevent a downward spiral into homelessness forcing decisions about what's legal, moral and ethical, or what is necessary to do for immediate survival?

All kinds of discussion could arise over these questions, and many would argue that each of us is totally responsible for making our decisions in life that in some way creates our own problems we are also totally responsible for.

But with a moneyfree society, few of those problems would exist, and no one should feel they have to choose robbery to survive and become a criminal as defined by law.

The idea of monetary accountability is visibly obvious to all of us because it affects us all in countless ways every moment of every day of our lives either directly or indirectly.

The most troublesome things about accountability over money often seem to be the stress and concern over having a reliable source of income to meet all financial obligations or having enough money to purchase something we think is extremely important to our well being.

Of course examples of these concerns are endless.

14 Monetary Accountability

The taxes we pay to support public assistance, social infrastructure or government projects can be acceptable or vexing depending on our attitude towards how these funds are distributed and used.

Often as not, most people seem to have some stress over paying taxes of any sort ranging from sheer frustration to simple inconvenience; or it may just be a psychological distaste at having to deal with 'big government'.

This is especially true when it comes to the annual ritual of filling out tax forms to verify fair payments to the federal and state government coiffeurs, which of course results in worry over additional taxes still due, or simply the hope that their tax returns will work out significantly in their favor.

For lower and middle income homeowners who have qualified for mortgages that can be paid as long as adequate income is available, there is much stress and concern when their source of income is threatened by a layoff, or when medical bills pile up unexpectedly.

So who is morally and ethically responsible for paying bills in these situations – the middle income homeowners, the corporate executives of the companies they work for, or something else not normally accounted for in the equation of monetary accountability?

Many business owners and managers seem to always have enough money to burn in their personal bank accounts yet can't seem to find it in their hearts or logic to take on the responsibility of adequately supporting their loyal employees who are not making enough to survive on

As we all know, any responsible employee could find themselves in dire circumstances if their income is suddenly cut off due to loss of their primary source such as a layoff due to little or no fault of their own.

Suppose a corporate exec has been morally and ethically responsible for doing his best to keep his company afloat, but still faces the imminent threat of bankruptcy due to lack of demand for the products they produce.

14 Monetary Accountability

In this case should an executive be held accountable to an employee facing a threat of a layoff if that layoff would trigger a home foreclosure due to a sudden loss of income, or should someone else be held accountable?

How about holding Congress accountable if they do not allocate funds for social programs to prevent homelessness, or if not Congress, then how about holding the system itself known as capitalism - responsible and accountable to have a safeguard to prevent these unnecessary situations?

Faced with the imminent threat of a foreclosure in the real world, a frantic scramble by a homeowner for additional sources of money to make up the difference often has no ready solution with the result that the bank holding their mortgage is not always willing to make adjustments.

If the bank holding the mortgage is unwilling to make adjustments for payments affordable to the homeowner to prevent a foreclosure, it is tempting to say that the bank is ethically and morally responsible to be held accountable to respond as to why they cannot help make it right.

Although some recent progress has been made in the way banks in general deal with foreclosures, many banks still resist the idea that foreclosures can be negotiated fairly for win-win solutions instead of forcing the foreclosures.

This happens because of the universal belief in the legality of the bottom line of monetary accountability that says no account can be allowed to go below zero no matter what the higher truth says is of greater priority to consider.

When trying to qualify for a loan to purchase a new home to gain peace of mind, freedom from environmental stress and generate some equity buildup, most house hunters seek a modest residence they can afford.

Most prefer a schedule of monthly payments to a bank as opposed to paying rent to a landlord in a questionably acceptable neighborhood, so they naturally try to engineer the outright purchase of their home with a deal they feel they can honestly afford and qualify for.

Many are turned down because their sources of income and credit history do not make the grade that banks decide is necessary for qualification due to the forced adherence of arbitrary financial accountability or 'credit worthiness' that is always considered top priority and not always consumer-friendly.

So often the ferocious tentacles of money accountability reach across illogical barriers and into every facet of living that affect and hurt those who can least afford to maintain the necessary funds to deal with it.

Considering the unfortunate spiral into homelessness, there are many reasons why a person may inevitably find themselves in this situation.

Sometimes the reasons are not apparent or traceable to choices that the homeless person could have avoided due to the effects of one's health regarding stress over money.

Whether we pay on a mortgage for our home or simply lease through monthly payments for rent, there is often the stress of maintaining the utility bills such as electricity, gas, water, sewer, and trash pickup, etc.

These bills of modern convenience living must be paid or the threat of shutoff on any of these services becomes an unavoidable result and may affect our health in ways not ordinarily understood or recognized.

Sometimes a homeowner will have any one or all of these necessary services shut off due to non-payment and then have to pay an additional fee for having them turned back on again thus adding unnecessary insult to injury.

Sometimes homeowners or renters could go through a cycle of having services shut off and back on again, and then having to pay the fee each time their service is back on after catch-up payments are satisfied.

The wasted time, effort and money affecting both the homeowner and the company due to lack of funds is an example of how non-compliance of the aggressive laws of financial accountability has such a hold on all of us.

Soon we may begin to question whether or not we are actually living in a civilized society, or possibly that the definition of 'civilized' has taken a cruel turn south.

For the average business person, the increasing threat of being sued by someone of higher authority over a decision that would normally be made innocently to help someone in financial need causes them to hold back and prevent them from acting on a moral obligation they would like to fulfill.

So common in our present day and age is the fear of possible litigation and entanglement with the law that gets in the way of the right thing to do or the ethical approach to help one's fellowman due to concern over one's reputation or potential obligation if a suite is successful.

For some less dramatic consequences, but situations that many face every day when paying for products or services on a timeline, there is the concern and inconvenience of the threat of late fees when bills are not paid on time.

Late fees are set up to not only fatten up profits for the fee inquisitors, but in the process force compliance on those who owe money regardless of extenuating circumstances.

Similar to late fees are the fees that banks charge for overdrafts that are sometimes inadvertent consequences of leading a busy life full of distractions that get in the way of normal responsibility to see that overdrafts do not occur.

Now consider the cost of college entrance fees and the costs for mandated educational materials in a civilized nation that had been the envy of the world for many generations and for many reasons involving opportunities for all.

Not only have the tuition costs for entering into a college or university in the U.S. often so prohibitive that only upper class families can afford to send their offspring, but the general cost of purchasing required accoutrements like books, clothing and fees, etc. adds to their misery.

14 Monetary Accountability

Many find that once accepted, they have to live with the stress of paying off burdensome education debts after they graduate and are ready to begin a normal and responsible family life on their own.

Adding insult to injury, there is no guarantee to see that all graduates are directed to employment opportunities they deserve for their time, money and energy spent in getting the proper education required for the skills that are always in demand throughout a healthy economy.

The legacy of monetary accountability has proven itself to be a deadly scourge for many and the primary reason why society cannot move ahead to a more sustainable future of freedom and abundance for all.

But the good news is that a solution is now being laid out in an ever so gradual step by step manner…

There is a viable alternative – a new way of thinking about the simple concept of moving into a sustainable moneyfree economy based upon the philosophy of 'value given for value earned'.

Although not new, the moneyfree way of doing business is an idea that until now has not been considered seriously enough; but one that could completely phase out and negate the whole concept of forced accountability that the money slave masters think is necessary in a civilized world society.

~15~
Educating the Population

Even though the idea of a moneyfree society seems such a worthy goal and ultra popular on the onset to the casual listener, many who think about it a bit deeper come up with immediate objections or serious doubt that it could actually work for a variety of reasons.

It seems logical to progressive thinkers that all of the reasons one could think of as to 'why it would not work' are based on biased thinking that moneyfree is too 'extreme' compared with the way the 'real' world of economics works.

At the forefront of that inherent bias is the lack of trust in one's fellowmen that such a massive cooperative effort to replace money with a workable alternative cannot happen due to an apparently unavoidable human nature of always wanting to take advantage of others if given the opportunity.

In other words, it is common belief that no one can trust anyone or anything that requires an immense change of thinking, especially when it has to do with money, the bread and butter issues surrounding money and the life blood flow of finance that most people hold sacred.

This results in a related myth that massive changes in the financial world would 'undoubtedly bring on problems of their own due to the perception of a global monetary system seemingly fraught with complexities, worry over security, and the fear of 'dire consequences' that it would all collapse if the trusted computer network controlling the functions would became irrevocably damaged or sabotaged.

Enter the concept of educating the masses regarding not only their fragile awareness of advantages inherent in a new economic system such as the moneyfree idea, but also a disposal of the myth that something so different from the traditional ways of doing business 'just wouldn't work'.

Like all other myths, this one would be based upon fear, and in this case mistrust of one's fellowmen which leads to the conclusion that we all need to compete for everything we deem of value in life.

In spite of the logic in favor of a revolutionary change, the widespread belief of the supremacy of money has so far trumped any serious effort to install any alternative that might prove far better for the common good..

Even the most progressive of activists who support the concept of moneyfree will have to admit that our complex financial system cannot be changed overnight.

Because of that, a suggestion comes to mind saying why not have realistic ways of educating the public that a series of steps can be arranged for necessary and logical changes in the immediate future to accomplish a desired journey from point A to point B.

Indeed, the suggestion bodes well that the process to ultimately eliminate money from the economy can unfold in a logical manner to demonstrate visible success that would be documented at each step along the way.

What if educational material regarding the concept of partial moneyfree systems could be included in a curriculum appropriate for every classroom from elementary schools on up through middle and high schools?

What if the faculties on school boards could actually embrace the idea that it would make good sense to teach the mechanics, the logistics and the logic of how our world society could benefit in so many ways when we change out thinking about the real purpose of money?

We have had businesses for many generations called nonprofit organizations that use surplus revenues to help achieve their goal and purpose instead of personal gain.

They try to eliminate the necessity of relying on profit for personal gain by using surplus income to successfully accomplish their mission, and by doing so remain content to rely on standard wages as adequate for personal needs.

They can often do so and be protected from the tax hawks who would otherwise have them contribute to tax revenues in the same manner as a business for profit must do, but thankfully they have the legal protection to control their surplus revenues to further their mission.

The decision to adopt a non-profit legal structure is one that will benefit any organization by taking away the pressure of the must earn profit motivation and replace it with a cooperative caring goal to contribute a product or service for the common good.

The result of ignoring the importance of profit goes hand in hand with a more general effort of transitioning to moneyfree living and eventually a totally global moneyfree economy, since the focus on strict monetary accountability is partially removed from their transactions.

Simple ideas can gradually phase out the old school way of doing business while phasing in logical alternatives that end the scourge of money accountability by systematically replacing it with cooperative systems that work equally well for everyone at all levels of economic net worth.

Educating the population in these and related ideas is an all-encompassing concept whose time has not only arrived, but has become an unstoppable wave and a logical financial destiny in the future for us all.

Methods of educating the public about a subject so 'off the wall' as moneyfree could easily be set up in classes appropriate for different ages and levels of understanding.

The educational methods and material to present could be chosen appropriately for all races, culture, background, philosophy of life and financial history, etc. and could be designed in several ways of approach.

Any approach used should probably have one focused priority to introduce related subjects that could help students appreciate why being free of money is logical and necessary to pursue, and how establishing the moneyfree idea could improve the quality of living for everyone in terms of true value regardless of their economic status.

Several thoughts come to mind regarding how classes can be set up as regular classroom agenda.

For example, teaching young people about not only the concept and definition of what moneyfree really means, but also the related levels of economic systems that would likely lead to complete freedom of money as we now know it.

An appropriate set of class presentations could be set up for the very young whose minds are still free of the potential baggage of, traditions, cultural norms, or hardened concepts taught in their upbringing about 'that's the way things work' or 'how life is supposed to operate'.

By keeping the goal of 'moneyfree' in mind, the most effective means to implement teaching concepts could be researched and then used in material for a natural way of helping students at any age acquire open-minded thinking about adjusting to the moneyfree idea in their adult years.

The purpose would be to uphold the real truth about how moneyfree should work to build trust and cooperation among all nations and cultures.

Class work could demonstrate how a logical approach can replace the myths, superstitions and mistrust that many people seem to develop as they face the status quo of doing business and experience the financial challenges of life.

A focused structuring of material presenting all the incongruence and dysfunctionality that occurs in a money-driven world could be put in the form of DVD presentations shown on monitors and TV screens in classrooms around the world.

This effort could then be followed with well-thought-out illustrations showing many dramatic examples of what can happen when the global economy is transformed into a moneyfree operation that works efficiently for everyone.

15 Educating the Population

This would involve not only a look at the end game of being completely moneyfree, but also demonstrate the fact that partial results along the way are more likely to lead to total success in due time by using a gradual approach and a logical implementation of changes in the way we think about money and how strict accountability is no longer necessary to do business in a more cooperative and efficient system.

All class presentations could be set up to illustrate how the transformations from the system they have presently to a more logical and user-friendly operation can occur naturally without question about how benefits of each advancement from the previous system becomes an improved reality.

For the very young starting out in elementary school, the use of animated cartoon style presentations could be put together to let them know how much fun it would be to live and operate without having to think about money.

And along with that idea, everyone would have more time to concentrate on the more important things in life like bonding with nature, developing new friends, taking care of pets and simply staying healthy.

The message would be that living a healthy prosperous lifestyle with their families without concerns over money can lead to the end game of being completely moneyfree, which would include benefits that many hardly ever think about..

Progressing to classrooms of students in high school, college and adult education, similar presentations using the same concepts with age-appropriate DVD media curricula is an idea whose time of arrival is now.

What better foundation of thought could be given than to point out the ramifications of a money-driven world so fiercely defended, even as a moneyfree existence is fiercely resisted by conservative bias at every opportunity?

We all know that the so-called elite world of the wealthy corporate heads and corrupt government officials driven by relentless conservative ideologies have effectively stifled growth and all efforts to level the economic playing field.

15 Educating the Population

It is time for average citizens to become educated on how they can relate to and support the full awareness of the beneficial side-effects of the moneyfree idea and how a moneyfree world will sooner or later be our future destiny.

A veritable plethora of approaches to public education can be instituted online and in classrooms for availability to all nations and cultures in the form of entertaining ads and documentaries recorded on DVDs and other media.

Support for a logical approach to independence from unnecessary concerns over money should provide for a step-wise approach to accomplish the end game of a new economy related to what the real purpose of money was assumed to be in the first place.

Beginning with where the perception of money begins in the minds of citizens, the concept of living without the need for strict accountability that says everyone must pay for everything they receive can be presented to children in entertaining video clips at home and in school classrooms as soon as they are old enough to understand money and why it is not always necessary for everything in life.

For example, a short movie on how children can get things they want in life by trading what they already have with others who simply want to exchange things to get something different is one idea that can be presented.

The purpose would be to compare how an acquisition of something important that they desire to have normally requires money, but can be obtained in other ways that are more sensible than holding to a strict money requirement.

As children advance in age and education, progressive material in the classroom can illustrate more reasons why money is not absolutely necessary for a successful life.

With a well-planned agenda each step along the way, by the time they are out of high school, they can have a well-rounded education and grounding in why removing money from the economy is truly a worthy goal to achieve.

131

15 Educating the Population

Loud and clear the school bell is ringing and the time has now come for dramatic changes in the way the public and our leaders think about the purpose of money and why money accountability is not as important as virtually all of us have been aggressively forced to conclude.

Using the aforementioned methods of educating the general population in each of the appropriate age levels, consider the step by step approach of partial changes designed to make the end result more understandable.

The first category of education could use appropriate methods at each age level including entertaining videos for children to understand the idea that subsistence basics for everyone is a necessary first step in easing away from strict monetary accountability.

The use of effective advertising and public seminars to continue the effort of educating the public about what happens when subsistence basics are held back from the needy would illustrate why it is so important to change the economic ebb and flow so that everyone benefits.

Next in line might be the concept of putting caps on maximum and minimum income, so it would make sense to have a series of classroom presentations using movie clips on DVDs and play acting to effectively illustrate the results of living with sensible caps on income compared with living life without them.

By having practical limits on maximum income as well as legal limits on how low minimum income can go seems so necessary that most common-sense folks should have no logical reason to question.

These approaches towards educating the population with special attention to the youth of all nations could be significant towards moving the concept of moneyfree in the right direction towards a successful conclusion.

By contrasting the benefits that can take place when relief from the stress of inadequate income is made the law

15 Educating the Population

of the land compared with what happens when funding is hoarded and prevented from flowing freely to where it is needed can be dramatically illustrated in many ways.

Considering educational material regarding expansion of the social umbrella, there could be a variety of statistical data available from existing socialistic regimes to put into convenient illustrations for class presentations at every age level to dramatically focus on the benefits.

Indeed, fairness, equality and efficiency in an existing compassionate society can show what happens whenever capitalistic control ignores the plight of the disadvantaged compared to what sensible compassionate socialism can do for Scandinavian countries and other nations.

Particular focus could be put on statistics that compare what expanding the social umbrella has accomplished as opposed to static regimes that are left to the buffeting of economic stress existing in a network of competition over money priorities typical of capitalism and dictatorships.

Using simple means of setting up educational material, another focus of presentations could tune in to the idea of what overall quality of life and living standards are like in existing moneyfree communities.

The lifestyles in these communities can be dramatically different from what many would be satisfied with in our consumer oriented existence, since most of us are locked into a complex variety of conveniences and resources that go way beyond a simple life living close to nature.

The process of educating the global population about a moneyfree existence could be managed with illustrations of a variety of actual living conditions that compare quality of life when the stress free advantages of living free from money transactions are compared to the concerns of those who spend much of their time geared to making enough money to pay bills or excess profit to control others.

Even though simply giving up the corporate business world in favor of simple holistic health living in a money-

133

free community has important advantages, any educational focus on comparing the two lifestyles should make it clear that available choices are not limited to these extremes.

Step by step changes in the way we think about money can ultimately create a united front taking the advantages of both extremes into one system that should work equally well for all citizens of any nation and culture.

One of my favorite subtopics in this story involves the Universal Monetary System that simply converts all forms of currency into a single monetary standard called a **sharo** (my suggestion) to replace all other forms of currency such as the dollar, the euro, yen, etc. that all require conversion when dealing with foreign money transactions.

With that in mind, the process of educating the public about the important step of establishing this goal prior to the end game of total moneyfree is a natural step, and can be done in a manner similar to the other step-wise topics of thinking in a more efficient and sensible manner.

All available resources and educational methods of teaching about steps leading to moneyfree could easily be prepared and brought together for each age level in ways that are entertaining as well as informative in their scope.

Once preliminary steps are taken that show significant progress towards putting the question of a truly universal monetary currency on the table for the global community to think about, I would suggest the next logical step to be the creation of an organization to handle the transactions of universal money that I call the ShareFlow Money Pool.

I see ShareFlow as a vitally important banking system that would work efficiently with a standard global currency set up as the basis of a universal monetary system.

Understanding the benefits of ShareFlow would logically follow after a track record of success occurs that involves public education about the preliminary steps leading up to it.

15 Educating the Population

Presentations could focus on ShareFlow's set up as a hack proof cybermoney standard to be used in a global economic free flow of currency that goes only to where it is needed.

Education of this nature would probably not seem so audacious and revolutionary as one might suspect at first.

To complete the educational process presented to the global population about how we can change our thinking about money, I suggest introducing the concepts defining a workable earned credit unit ECU network that makes sense if this concept was not presented previously in the preliminary work needing to be accomplished.

Even though the use of earned credit units in an ECU global network would be a monumental aberration in how we normally think about money, proper education could once again lead to the icing on the cake that awaits in the end game of a truly moneyfree way of living.

To correctly define a moneyfree society in a sensible way, the ECU network would provide freedom from the slavery of concerns about bill payments, while creating an audacious but efficient way of doing business in a world where most of us might like to think about other things not related to financial accountability.

~16~
Phasing out Money

Once the SANE Economy is working as required by design and implementation, the advantages of operating moneyfree in the sense of reduced monetary transactions and the gradual phasing out of the accountability factor that goes with it should begin to make itself known loud and clear throughout the global community.

Indeed it should be very apparent to all who would still think it was necessary to depend upon the money-driven accountability idea in order to earn a secure and comfortable lifestyle and supposedly keep the economy from collapsing.

Even with a SANE (Socially Automated Network Economy) way of doing business, there still might be hard core conservatives hanging on to the idea that we must prevent anyone from getting a 'free handout they don't deserve' because they may not have 'worked hard' for the necessities of life that the wealthy supposedly have done.

But once the advantages of cooperation and trust that make life better for everyone are apparent, the next step along the way towards moneyfree operations could be to reduce the importance of money accountability in ways to negate fraud and hoarding of assets.

This effort can be given a boost by way of negating the traditional motivation of being competitive and replacing competition with cooperation to support a beneficial social umbrella that does not depend upon business profit at the unnecessary expense of others.

While phasing out the other unnecessary money-driven transactions accompanied with the acceptance of a totally different philosophy about how we think about money, the gurus of the business world should begin to realize that it is becoming more desirable to operate via a more cooperative way of doing business as evidenced by a successful track record of activity in the SANE economic system.

Benefits to the masses including the wealthy elite and many hard core conservatives should clearly demonstrate a free-up of more personal time and energy for attention to other issues in life that do not involve concerns inherent with traditional accountability of money.

Once again, it does not take a rocket genius to realize that a gradual rise in the standard of living for everyone would include even the 1% who thought their accumulation of money alone would be their only goal worth striving for.

During the process of reducing the importance of profit and monetary accountability, transactions involving money could be gradually phased out on many levels.

By adding more designations of necessary goods and services under the SANE economic umbrella, the phase-out process would continue to evolve and be able to periodically identify new products and services considered inclusive as reasonable standards for everyone.

Examples of a gradual phase-out could include various goods and services obtained by way of automatic transfers of funds to personal accounts such as the subsistence basics of food, clothing, shelter, basic health care, cost of public transportation, cost of communication, the postal system, home energy usage, water and other utilities, etc.

The various items of commerce that would still be paid with manual transactions might include the purchasing of all higher priced items such as various specialty versions of the previous list of basics plus all other goods and services not considered as true necessities.

As minimum standards and quality of living generally improve for the masses, other items from the list of non-basics can be added gradually under the SANE umbrella of auto-payment using personal accounts in ShareFlow that would replace manual monetary transactions.

Over time, the evolution of the global SANE economy would continue to phase out the traditional use of money and accountability of funds in a way that would eventually lead to a complete phase-over for all goods and service transactions that are logically identified as necessities.

Under the SANE economic system in full operation, every-day transactions would be virtually free of the usual money-accountability concerns without further need for the average citizen to spend a lot of time and energy thinking about having enough money to pay bills.

Universal issues over money transactions are always twofold, which of course involve concerns about having enough funds to pay for the necessities, and in so doing must never allow one's bank account to fall below zero in available balance in order to avoid costly add-on fees.

As we all know, any account that falls below zero in available funds inevitably leads to add-on fees that are imposed by rules made up by bankers who control monetary input and output without regard to their customers' ability to always maintain adequate deposits.

Although add-on fees are supposed to be applied only for the cost of handling transactions, often the fees are quite exorbitant and do not reflect justification to profit from the shortfall of customers who may be struggling to maintain adequate income, or may have inadvertently overdrawn their accounts due to the distractions of everyday living.

To phase out money completely from a firmly rooted money-driven world would of necessity take an immense effort of providing education, time, money and intelligent planning to arrive at the final goal.

The steps leading to the end game can be identified up front and be talked about in the forum of public education.

When that happens, the participants could help state a definitive awareness that money and money accountability are not really necessary processes that give anyone any real benefit to themselves in terms of the important issues that define true quality of life.

Indeed, our global society has already taken some very basic steps toward that end without even realizing it such as electronic currency gadgets and their associated transactions involving the concepts of efficient transfer of funds from one account to another.

Other steps along the way include easier ways to buy things with credit, auto-payment of bills, easier payoff of some debts, the gifts to charity, the acquisition of invisible money through investments and the avoidance of money entirely through volunteer work, barter and trade, etc.

The almost universal use of credit and debit cards in today's method of handling spot purchasing at the source of acquisition makes visible money even less visible by allowing the payments of bills to occur in cyberspace with less effort and time spent in the thought process.

The use of cybermoney works well for everyone as long as everyone has adequate income to support the intended process of value received for value earned.

This becomes abundantly clear even though we all know that our accounts are automatically debited each time we allow our monthly payments to be taken out.

With so many ways to use auto-transactions, many of us with a sustainable income do not have to think about the mechanics of paying bills as much as we used to.

By not having to consciously think about money as much as was necessary in times past, many average citizens are actually one step closer to the end game.

Auto-payments make it inherently easier to accept the moneyfree idea since the time and energy normally taken up with thinking about monetary involvement can be used for the more valued issues of daily living.

Unfortunately for the majority of low-income and the poverty stricken, these conveniences do not work for them since their entire livelihood often depends upon survival and struggle for acquiring enough money to buy the subsistence basics and/or pay off their increasing debt.

The SANE economic umbrella would eliminate that problem by having all the basics of life logically prioritized for availability to all without exception, net worth, status or circumstances normally used for disqualification.

Over the years, payments of income and sales taxes have been modified many times to allow a more automatic means of transfer of funds that can occur without time and energy focused on the actual transfers taking place in cyberspace.

By not having to think about the process of transfer of money in any situation, we are automatically one step closer to the concept of money free as long as our accounts are systematically fed periodically to hold sufficient funds to cover all necessary transactions at any time day or night.

Charity drives always make the donors of funds, goods or services think about what they are donating which means money in most cases that the recipients of the charity can accept as partial relief from being accountable for every transaction in terms of payback defined by the normal 'value given for value received' requirement.

Volunteer work is obviously a direct statement against the money-driven concept by providing a clear example of a need fulfillment that sidesteps strict adherence to a money transaction, yet benefits both the giver and receiver.

Traditionally any volunteer work performed in abstract ways can motivate the donors and the recipients to gratefully accept the entire process without worry of financial stress or inconvenience of having to account for any gain or loss.

At the other end of the financial spectrum we have the world of investments where those who have the means in terms of sustained income to their accrued net worth can leverage their money to increase their wealth by investing in stocks, bonds and commodities as they see fit.

Even though there is no guaranteed outcome for gain or minimized loss in any investment, most benefit from this continuous money game by learning to call their shots in an intelligent, clever or informed manner.

But investments are a manipulation of money that does not measure worth in terms of a direct or readily definable philosophy of value received for value earned involving the brokers.

By default, investments are devices that complicate the lives of some due to the imposition of unwarranted portions of time and energy used in the often complex money games whose sole purpose is usually set to simply increase one's net worth without any concern for a direct benefit to society.

For those who live a comfortable lifestyle that sidesteps the money game of investments entirely, they have perhaps unknowingly taken 'one small step for man' and in so doing, 'one giant step for mankind'.

And even if inadvertently not aware of that, they place themselves at the forefront of a sustainable future no longer dependent upon the use of money to be their salvation or their necessity for the creation of whatever they consider as their true values in life.

~17~
Earned Credit Units

With a global economy as defined in previous chapters called SANE (the (Socially Automated Network Economy) becoming fully operational, it will presumably bode well and operate securely, equitably and successfully for all citizens via the lifeblood of an efficient monetary distribution using the ShareFlow Money Pool.

This is tantamount to having a healthy circulation of money with money accountability that finally makes sense in an otherwise complex global economic system.

As envisioned in more detail, it could work equally well for all civilized nations, cultures and ideologies throughout the global environment where everyone wins regardless of economic status, race, gender, philosophy, background or ethnic origin one happens to be.

Indeed it is a fair assumption that a SANE economic revolution or something close to it could raise the standard of living and free up the average citizen from the stress and drudgery of being held as virtual slaves to money and the accountability of strict adherence to payment of bills.

It is logical to assume that such a system would be the nirvana of economics that many progressives have dreamed about, except for one major loophole in security that the SANE concept as presently defined would not dispose of.

As efficient and magnificent as the SANE system might be even by using money as money was meant to be used, it could not guarantee freedom from abuse or fraudulent use.

In fact it would still be vulnerable to the imbalances that disreputable managers, corporate heads and politicians, not to mention the average dishonest citizenry in the operations of money transactions would invariably use to find ways to circumvent the original intent and find ways to acquire funds for unethical purposes.

Any unethical or fraudulent purpose could ultimately be converted into some type of control mechanism at one level or another to keep others in a state of partial slavery albeit not nearly as severe as would exist without SANE reforms.

Indeed, many improvements leading to a truly fair and equitable system working for everyone could logically be brought about when the entire SANE economic overhaul working as a coordinated system was in full operation.

Even if only one SANE subsystem working in tandem with a universal currency was in operation on a global scale, we could expect significant improvements leading to an end game that would operate equally well for all citizens.

Because of that reality, the next logical step must now be identified, defined and introduced in a way that suggests that the SANE concept using seven subsystems would be the logical and necessary first major overhaul in preparation for the final death of money.

With sufficient public support for implementation, the SANE system would have to be ultimately phased into an even more radical challenge designed to make the subject of money accountability totally obsolete

In fact it would have to be done in a secure manner so that hoarding or dishonest acquisition of monetary gain by any citizen, business, corporation or government would not be physically or even technically possible.

It would have to be well-planned so that there would be no possibility of some loophole discovered along the way to allow unregulated free exchange of money between citizens that would create the beginnings of a new gap similar to what we now call the gulf between the haves and the have-nots in the global community.

Enter the concept of issuing and using earned credit units instead of money as presently defined being the lifeblood of the global economy that handles all transactions involving, wages and payments for goods and services.

Let us define the earned credit unit to replace money as equal to one **yuna** designated for use as either singular or plural, and having a value to be explained shortly.

In the strictest sense, the concept of earned credit units still functions as money, but would be a totally new system that completely changes the way we think about money.

And unlike the SANE economy I have described using **sharo** as the unit for money, rules could be prescribed in the revised system to assure that 'value given for value earned' is adhered to as a function of the way the earned credit units defined as **yuna** are used and how they are issued.

A case can be made for allowing earned credit units to be issued directly to the gainfully employed as 'value given for value earned' instead of allowing money to transfer to privately controlled government, corporation and business accounts where it is still subject to mismanagement at the expense of the workers.

Indeed it is logical that **yuna** should be issued directly, and only to the workers who earned them in accordance with their contributory value defined by their employment status and benefit to the common good.

This requirement makes earned credit units independent of the requirement that businesses, corporations and the government must have profit controlled money in their accounts to be able to make wage payments or purchases.

Unlike units of money however, the use of earned credit units in the revised SANE economy defined as YUNA would have the means of disallowing anyone to transfer them to any other person's account either willingly or through theft or fraud because yuna would only be issued directly to the workers that have earned them by reason of their employment status.

17 Earned Credit Units

This would guarantee that earned credit units could only be used by wage earners who earned them for purposes tied directly to personal transactions for products and services.

The concept is certainly not new, but revolutionary in the sense that many people now living are so steeped with an indelible' rock-hard requirement of checks and balances for monetary discipline that they might quickly pass it off by calling it 'entirely unworkable'.

Fortunately a strong case can be made that an earned credit unit economy as compared to what we normally think of as money would have a logical way of proving itself out as a practical medium of exchange once proper groundwork to educate the masses would have been previously presented as part of a curriculum of public education.

It would seem that discussing the advantages of using earned credit units instead of traditional money could be intelligently planned for the purpose of general education classes, advertising, and the use of word of mouth incentives to talk about an idea whose time has come.

Discussions could center on the original intent of money being a medium of fair exchange that could be redefined as a very practical alternative in the form of earned credit units given out only to those who are qualified by reason of their useful employment to themselves and to society in general.

What then is an earned credit unit (a **yuna**) all about, and how can it work if issued only to wage earners?

As I see it, the universal money pool I call ShareFlow would morph into using **yuna** to replace all forms of the previous units of money I referred to as **sharo**, but would still be resident in cyberspace for use in all transactions involving wages, salaries and prices for goods and services.

Credit units would be issued only to individuals who are recognized and qualify as gainfully employed in their profession which in itself would first have been analyzed and qualified as contributing to the common good.

145

17 Earned Credit Units

All earned credit units would be issued in accordance with the philosophy of value given for value earned, with a clear emphasis and understanding of the word 'earned'.

But unlike money as we now think of it, **yuna** would not be allowed to transfer from one personal account to another but must be used only by the person who received the credits for purchasing necessary goods and services.

This simple rule is very far reaching as it disallows the hoarding of money since **yuna** would be issued only on the basis of one's employment, and by law could only be used as payment in exchange for products or services that are needed by that individual.

These two stipulations effectively prevent any other person from acquiring credits they did not earn and would negate the need to be accountable for future use because they would be removed from active purchasing status and become archived as evidence of past transactions.

Archiving spent **yuna** would convert them to a new status for the purpose of keeping track of past transactions with the business they were used at, and thus disappear from use in future transactions or in unauthorized transfer to personal accounts where they were not earned..

Furthermore, any occupation or business by definition would be qualified on the basis of how it can contribute to the welfare of the common good where everyone else in the global community would benefit directly or indirectly as a result of work performed by an employed person.

Employment status would be defined as pertaining to responsible labor at a specified level of value, but could exclude some forms of work traditionally considered as a job, but in the new system might be disqualified if the 'job' was not contributing to the welfare of the common good in some meaningful way.

To illustrate how earned credit units would work, let us consider those at the lower end of wage compensation due to traditionally low-paying employment who have had to struggle for enough income, salary or compensation to earn enough to pay for the essentials of subsistence.

Although the SANE economy as defined in previous chapters would eliminate most of the inequities between the wealthy and the lower classes, it would have to do that by using new rules of distribution and accountability to correct persistent problems in a troubled system.

As set up that way, it would still be open to potential fraudulent or unethical activity that would invariably result in hoarding of net worth either legally or illegally.

Anytime hoarding occurs in an otherwise free flowing monetary system, it effectively removes part of the tools of commerce (efficient flow of money) leaving the entire system deficient for maximum efficiency that is supposed to provide balance and equity for the common good.

All earned credit units by definition and by necessary rules stipulation would be issued on the basis of useful employment in any qualified occupation, and could be set up for issue on an arbitrary but timely basis.

Salary and wage rates would not be based upon how much company profit or quality of work is accomplished by each employee, but simply issued via the qualification of what kind of employment and level of responsibility each worker is officially set up to do as a result of being a hired average-valued worker of a business, a corporation, a government or simply being self-employed.

The number of **yuna** to be issued as wages would be decided in advance by standards tied to the description of each position of employment only, and be issued equitably as long as a worker continues to hold that position of trust and employment in a responsible manner.

In other words, **yuna** would be issued to all gainfully employed workers no matter what occupation they are in as long as their work continues to accomplish some kind of benefit to society and contribute to the common good.

147

17 Earned Credit Units

The issuance of earned credit units to all employees would be accomplished through an automated procedure, but would not allow transfer of units from any individual to another individual that would circumvent the system of having active earned credit units paid only to the accounts of workers who have actually earned them.

This means that the concept of money as we now know it to function would be eliminated from the global economy entirely, because **yuna** would be dispensed as 'value given for value earned' and could be used only by the recipients for purchase of goods or services.

After being used once to purchase goods or services, the specific credit units involved in the transactions would be set aside as ineligible for further use to buy anything else, but would be put in separate accounts available for ShareFlow to use as evidence of the business transactions and qualification of the businesses to be seen as viable and worthy to continue their operations.

The issuance of **yuna** for wages and salaries would be a new process to what was formerly known as a universal money system such as ShareFlow and what could now be called the ShareFlow Earned Credit Unit Network and be referred to simply as ShareFlow

With an earned credit unit system in operation, there would no longer be loans given out for any kind of credit and debt accountability since there would no longer be borrowing necessary as part of the economic energy flow.

Taking over for what would have previously operated simply as a universal money pool could still retain the name of ShareFlow, but its function would now be much simpler in that it would operate as a free flow of credit units available for allocation to wage earners, without the requirement of payback as taxes.

As a simple example, let's say Cybertron Electronics pays an average of 1000 earned credit units per week to each worker at a certain level of employment qualification measured in terms of value to society in general.

Sally Martin who works for Cybertron has an account with ShareFlow that keeps track of her 1000 **yuna** salary and resultant expenses for products and services.

On a certain day each week she goes to Valley Grocers to purchase her needs for the week and has the checker deduct the cost in **yuna** from her account.

At checkout, Sally hands her **yuna** account verification card (similar to an ordinary debit card) so that 42 **yuna** can be taken out to pay for her groceries.

Where does the 42 **yuna** go? – They would go into the store's transaction account where they are deactivated for further use as 'transaction money'.

They are stored there as needed to verify to ShareFlow that the store is successful as a business, but those **yuna** cannot be taken out for further use since they have done their work to give a customer her groceries as fair trade for a 'value given for value earned' transaction.

ShareFlow does not need to collect them for future transactions since its function is to dispense credit units to wage earners directly from what could be called an **'infinite ocean'** that does not depend upon tax payback.

The store does not need them because the store (just like every other business) has no bills to pay.

All of their employees are on the same system of credit units issued from ShareFlow as a function of 'value given for value earned'.

In the next chapter we will take a look at how a global economy could work using the earned credit unit basis for transactions to replace all traditional forms of money and complexity of monetary accountability that goes with it.

~18~
The ECU Network

Since we live in a more globalized economy now, it is natural to expect that a workable system geared to operate for the good of all could eventually be extracted out of the existing economies of nations so that every country could benefit significantly as compared to doing nothing.

It would seem logical that the preference of citizens with at least average intelligence would not resist supporting their leaders to work together to form a cooperative to include all nations to standardize operations for a unified and optimum way to handle financial transactions.

Once a standardized unit of currency quantification has been agreed upon that replaces all other forms of currency and can be stored electronically in a hack-free cyberspace, why should there be significant resistance?

Money would take on a revised meaning in the form of digital quantification of earned credit units for value in every government, corporate, business and personal account of every nation operating as a universal trading partner.

It would be a modification of the ShareFlow money pool by replacing ShareFlow cybermoney with credit units.

ShareFlow would be the new universal banking system known as the ECU credit unit network, and would adapt operations for each nation into a standard cooperative of replacing money with earned credit units.

And it would be a natural to eventually include all nations under the ECU Network phase-over from a money based system to an earned credit unit based system only.

The entire process might take some time to finalize depending upon the magnitude of complexities that each nation would face, but ultimate success could be assured by giving the population of each nation incentives to complete the task in a timely manner.

The ramifications of a ShareFlow ECU network become enormous as soon as all the factors that contribute to the beneficial results are identified, advertized and promoted to dispel any doubts and create trust in one's neighbor to work together in a mutual cooperative.

Whatever objections that exist should be relatively easy to overcome in favor of increased cooperation resulting in a global enterprise that could include 3rd world countries since their economies would stand to benefit the most.

Each nation would have the opportunity to function in a manner that would phase itself towards an end game for the global community to encompass all nations, all cultures and all localities to permanently end the money-driven system of slavery to money accountability that we now experience.

In the meantime, the entire global economy could be operating under a SANE system as described previously, where all forms of money would be converted to universal currency with a standardized unit so that ShareFlow could work equally well anywhere.

With ShareFlow, every transaction would use standard units that could be electronically moved out of the infinite ocean of cybermoney to go only to those who deserve it and to where it can do the most for the common good.

Under the revised SANE system, the entire concept of earned credit units would be equivalent to a virtual state of numbers on all types of personal, business, corporate and government accounts within ShareFlow that are designed to function securely and transparently in every transaction.

All goods and services throughout the global network could be assigned their value in whole numbers of **yuna** as my suggestion for the credit unit name, and would no longer resort to the unnecessary inconvenience of using fractions of units to cover strict accountability in value.

18 The ECU Network

By accepting **yuna** in integral numbers without using fractions of the base unit, we create an efficiency that would operate similarly to the way quantum mechanics in physics is depicted as using integral numbers for particle and wave interactions.

All a consensus would have to do is adjust the value of the **yuna** to a reasonable standard set at the approximate value of a least expensive item.

Then adjustments can be made to adequately assign in whole number units the net worth for all wages, salaries, products and services throughout the global economy.

The result of implementing the ECU Network would then negate all existing money for future transactions and accountability such as taxation, credit, debt, investments, stocks and bonds, gold, silver, checks, credit cards, cash, coins, money orders and essentially the whole ball of wax regarding money manipulations as we now know them.

With ShareFlow as defined in earlier chapters, money might still be hoarded by those with unethical motivation, however by limiting all financial transactions to use earned credit units instead of money, those problems are totally eliminated by disallowing transfer for unethical purposes.

By issuing credit units to every employed worker in the global economy, the new medium and associated rules of operation replace the concept of traditional financing to a more advanced operation in that earned credit units could never be transferred from one person to another.

Once earned credit units are issued to wage earners in accordance with pre-determined quantities on the basis of the value of each type of gainful employment that exists, there would need to be hack-proof firewalls and other means of security put in place to disallow transfer of units to any other person who did not earn them.

The rule would be that once issued to an individual, that specific individual owns those units until they are paid out and accounted for in exchange for value received for value earned on personal products or services.

Electronic personal and business tablets once referred to as electronic currency tablets could be redefined so as to reflect the evolution away from money to the system of earned credit units that replace traditional money and be known as earned credit unit tablets (ECUT's).

Instead of having to use any conventional means for payment transactions, the ShareFlow ECU network could automate all transaction information to be conveniently displayed on a customer's personal ECUT for any type of monetary transaction.

They could display personal ShareFlow bank accounts that an account holder is qualified to access for account information, however any transaction itself may require only a transaction card called an employment status card (ESC) that verifies the owner's identity and is used in a manner similar to the way ordinary debit cards are used.

An ECUT would not have to be accessed at the points of transaction involving purchases of goods and services because actual transactions would be authorized directly with an ESC employment status card that could debit the proper number of credit units from a customer's personal account within the ShareFlow ECU network.

Every global citizen could have one or more personal ECUTs along with an ESC card (taking the place of cash, credit cards, check books and other debit cards, etc.

Every business would record purchase transactions in a manner similar to the way debits of money transactions from a traditional account are accomplished.

For every purchase transaction at a point of sale, the business would transfer the appropriate number of earned credit units from the customer's account to the business account where they are deactivated and are locked in place

Once that happens, all spent credit units are disallowed

for transfer to any other account including the accounts of the business owners and their employees.

The stored credit units in a business account could not be transferred to any personal account but would be held as evidence that the store is successful in selling their products or services and to the degree their success is determined.

Once it is acknowledged that a business has a reasonable number of credit units stored in the account representing past transactions, these units can disappear because their work has been accomplished in providing a fair exchange of value given for value earned in terms of purchased goods or services to their customers.

Every business stays in operation by showing a viable account measure of proof of purchases and does not need to depend on profit from sales, because the purpose of the business is then validated and qualified to have an X number of reliable employees who would then continue to get their earned credit units directly from ShareFlow every month.

For convenient budget analysis purposes, every ECUT might look similar to an ordinary calculator, smart phone, or IPod held in the hand, pocket or purse.

ECUT tablets would allow customers to review their account balance for determining their affordability to buy something at a certain cost, and would also function to display the real time value of their current net worth in various subdivisions of categorical spending.

An ECUT tablet would display a customer's net worth defined by the number of earned credit units that exist in their personal account as well as the number of units taken out of their account after a purchase.

For general purchase of goods and services, customers would need their employment status ESC cards kept in a wallet or purse to present for authorizing transactions at the time of purchase, and optionally an ECUT tablet to display their account balances and affordability to spend.

All tablets could have a convenient screen display for every applicable account owned by an individual who is buying something or accepting purchase for something.

For a business owner authorizing monthly wages for their employees, an ECUT could also function as a way of keeping track of how many credit units are authorized for payment out of ShareFlow to each employee.

By issuing wages, salaries or payments for any work accomplished, ShareFlow itself is the paymaster.

Every worker and business owner would get paid as an employee and only as an employee from ShareFlow for work performed in accordance with the value of the work they accomplish for the benefit of the common good.

Every time an earned value transaction for purchase is accomplished, it may involve two ECUTs used, with one showing the transfer of **yuna** from a customer's personal account, and the other recording the transaction in terms of **yuna** received by the business in their account.

The credit units in the business accounts are kept there as part of the qualification process to allow wage payments to employees of the business and to qualify the approved number and types of workers needed for employment in each business location.

Result: Customers give up a certain amount of earned credit units transferred from their personal accounts to appropriate business accounts while they get the benefit of receiving goods and services paid for in earned credit units plus a record of the transactions.

The entire ShareFlow network is assumed to have adequate backup capabilities using foolproof redundant user ID and password coding to disallow any possibility of serious errors or hacking of any account.

Every transaction would be recorded with the code numbers of both the buyer and the seller involved in any transaction, and would be redundantly set up within all global banks in the universally accepted financial network to track any error or attempted hacking in case records are lost at any one location.

The whole concept of the ShareFlow ECU network would be based upon a simple philosophy and assumption that whoever deserves credits for work done in terms of their status as an employee receives them directly from ShareFlow on a periodic basis (typically monthly).

Since the usual procedures of using money would no longer exist in this new system, whoever does not deserve anything greater than a specific number of earned credits would not get them until they are earned.

This means that no one could receive unearned credit units and hoard them for purposes of control over others, and no one could significantly benefit fraudulently even if they were to try to use a lost or stolen ESC card.

All business owners and their employees would be automatically disallowed to transfer credit units from their business account to any personal account, since that type of transaction would be coded as illegal and stopped by comparison of accounts before it could occur.

Likewise, any person or business offering products or services to a customer would not have a lot of incentive to transfer unqualified credit units to a personal account, since that person's interest in adequate income would be satisfied by the number of credit units legally dispensed as a result of whatever their personal employment status is rated at to be a useful contribution to the welfare of the common good.

Keeping in mind that all earned credit units originate in the ShareFlow global network and would be dispensed only to qualified employee personal accounts as determined by business account wage and salary authorization, let us look at several examples of how it would work depending on the type of business involved.

With a self-employed and sole proprietor being the only employee of a business, one could operate with one account that becomes simultaneously considered a business and a personal account in the ShareFlow banking system.

Since there are no other employees in the business, this account could suffice as his personal wage dispensation as well as his personal earned credit unit account with separate subdivisions by virtue of his sole proprietorship.

When earned credit units are debited from his personal allotment issued from ShareFlow, the debited units become inactive for further spending and are relocated accordingly to the various business accounts he deals with in exchange for goods and services he receives.

Likewise, all credit units paid to him as a sole proprietor from clients he deals with for purchase of his products or services could be transferred to his business account subdivision that keeps a record of how well his business is doing and acts as justification that his business is legitimate and is successful enough to stay in operation.

Examples of this type of employment include artists, musicians, consultants, professional volunteers, students, handymen, authors, home operated businesses and any others that could be classified as self employed.

The next example is for a small business hiring several other employees that are authorized for payment of earned credit units from ShareFlow by virtue of their employment with the business they work for.

The owner gets a standard monthly allotment of credit units placed into a business account on ShareFlow for the payout of wages to his or her pre-qualified employees.

These employees would get paid directly by ShareFlow with the correct number of earned credit units allocated for each employee and dispensed to their personal accounts.

Each business would have a separate account or subdivision of one account that accepts payments of earned credit **yuna** from their customers which is then used to verify that the business is operating successfully and is thus qualified to continue authorizing wages from ShareFlow.

Since the owner is also an employee of the business, he or she can only use **yuna** for personal purchases out of their personal account, and therefore cannot access **yuna** already spent by customers that is deactivated and placed separately in the business account.

A similar arrangement would exist for farmers, ranchers and others in the agricultural business, since they can act either as sole proprietors or hire workers who receive wages by virtue of a qualified business account.

However large a business is, the earned credit units are dispensed directly from ShareFlow after their authorization is verified by ShareFlow's business qualification team.

Whether a business is small or large, the whole idea is to allow every business to have two separate account types in the ShareFlow system.

One type is for issuing wages to the employees, and the other is to accept payments from customers for verification that their business is operating successfully.

Customers purchasing goods and services spend their previously earned credit units in exchange for value received at the time of purchase, with the spent **yuna** going into the store's business account and flagged inactive.

Once ShareFlow reviews accounts holding expired yuna, the yuna disappear and are no longer needed since their work and reason for existence has been accomplished.

CEO's of corporations are put into the same category as any other employee of their company, except of course their personal wages would be allocated appropriately higher than the average worker, but not out of line with the true value of what they actually contribute to the common good.

Government workers are employees of the government they work for whether it is local, state or federal, so there would be no basic difference in the way their organization is funded or in the way employees are paid out of ShareFlow.

This would include even the military and the president on down through all public office holders, with each being paid according to their employment status and qualifications in terms of contributions to the common good.

To summarize, the ShareFlow ECU Network would exist as an advanced foundation for the SANE economy having the purpose of paying workers throughout the global economy with earned credit units instead of money.

The major differences in earned credit units compared to traditional money that we now use would be two-fold:

Earned credit units would be issued to wage earners as compensation for the work they perform according to their employment status and could not be transferred to any other person's personal account but must be used and spent only by the person who earns and receives them.

With an ECU Network enhancement of the universal money pool previously described, no taxes would need to be collected because the ShareFlow universal banking system would operate with a virtual infinite ocean of credit units to draw from for payment to all personal accounts as qualified wages earned by reason of 'value given for value received'.

As a result, all traditional concepts involving 'national debt' or even personal debt would then become archaic and would no longer exist at any level.

~19~
Politics without Money

In the previous chapter, earned credit units are defined as the basis of an economy operating without money, yet for most, the belief remains that the only way to do business in a successful economy is to continue to rely on traditional money and money accountability as we know it.

Earned credit units used in lieu of visible dollars and cents would on the onset appear to be just another form of money, and of course based upon the prevailing view of how money implies accountability of funds, there would be no question that it should be considered as such.

In the status quo of financial accountability, very few question that some form of money will always be required due to the age-old belief that human nature is permanently ingrained with the attitude of something like - 'That's the way things are done and it can never be changed'.

Earned credit units defined as the standard of exchange share the same definition regarding accountability of getting value received for value earned in the same manner as the use of dollars and cents is supposed to imply; however most other comparisons between how the two systems are used is like comparing black and white or night and day.

In a certain sense both systems could still be thought of as equivalent by those who can't let loose of the idea of money and the resultant accountability associated with all monetary transactions, however earned credit units will differ with traditional money in several ways that are very different from the way money is being used and changed into something else that many had never intended.

160

19 Politics Without Money

Let us think of the concept of moneyfree in a relative sense that takes on real meaning the more we understand the true ramifications of not having to concern ourselves with having money for paying bills, purchasing necessities or using it for anything else we think we need in life.

One crucial difference between money as it is now used compared to the way earned credit units could be used is simply the understanding that credit units would be issued only to workers engaged in useful employment on the basis of value given for value earned.

In this instance, the word 'earned' is the core word that is needed to measure how well the type of work in any specific job designation would benefit the common good in order to determine qualified numbers of earned credit units to be paid to employees in each specified type of work.

By understanding the word 'earned' as the core word for all transactions involving wages, salaries or payments for products or services needed for everyday living, we are in a sense separating the wheat from the chaff in respect to how economics is supposed to operate.

The system for issuing and accounting for payment of earned credit units should exclude issuing units for any other purpose including unnecessary hoarding by the wealthy, fraudulent acquisition, or the unethical methods that many political machines use for power and control of the voters.

In other words, earned credit units as envisioned in this story would not be transferable to anyone else once they are issued to the work force of individuals on the basis of their gainful employment with respect to the common good.

Once issued in wages or salaries to specific employees, they would then become available only for the purpose of spending appropriately to handle costs of necessary goods and services required by the wage earners.

Earned credit units once issued to an individual are tied to that individual and are given up only when that person

161

turns them in for fair exchange resulting in the acquisition of necessary products and services.

Operating as the ShareFlow ECU network using **yuna** as the standard earned credit unit, this system would be set up to use transfer coding to negate transfer of **yuna** to any business, government or political entity since none of those facilities would have taken part in the earning process.

Another important difference between earned credit units and money as we know it today is that the ingrained concept of taxation would be totally eliminated in favor of a transaction system where the simple philosophy of 'value given for value earned' is the driving force of a free flow of credit units to everyone qualified by ShareFlow.

This changes the way money is used in a very dramatic way because it constrains the world of finance to use credit units only to accomplish something of true necessity, thus abolishing the need of profit and wealth as the measure of success in any business, corporation or government.

One way money is wasted is with excessive advertising because much of the purpose of advertising is to convince potential customers to purchase goods and services they often do not need for an optimum quality of living.

How far our society has come from the original concept of purpose seems unimaginable, because it is quite apparent that much time and energy is spent in financial matters and wasteful spending that seriously drags down the efficiency and life blood of the global economy.

It is obvious to many of average intelligence that far too much money is hoarded by bankers and corporations who can then influence voters to elect unethical politicians who slant laws in their favor and thus ignore the original purpose money was designed for.

With the earned credit unit system that disallows money from ending up in the hands of politicians, we can visualize a new kind of economy operating without the inefficiencies of having specific occupations to keep track of unnecessary and often unethical transfers of money to those who have not earned it and do not deserve it.

Now let's take a closer look at how money in politics has corrupted what could have been a fair, equitable, efficient and well ordered system called capitalism, and how criminals have been allowed to circumvent the system and acquire unearned money in a plethora of different ways.

Many stay within the limits of legality, yet still manage to increase their wealth disproportionately by taking unfair advantage of others having significantly less to start with.

Many inherit vast sums of money for leverage to easily increase their wealth so they can take over positions of power in business, corporations and government.

With inordinate wealth to begin with, many unethically use manipulation and legal transfers according to the rules of investment or other means without any thought of having earned their dues through useful labor or value produced.

Having a large accrual of wealth gives business owners the means to pressure everyone to pay for subsistence basics whether they have adequate income or not, and thus they easily create a severe imbalance between those with adequate income and many who have to struggle for their basics.

Politics by definition started out as an acceptable activity designed to identify and support the individuals chosen for nomination and election to various offices of responsibility in government at every level.

Politics at all levels has clearly evolved into a horrendous control mechanism fueled by the acquisition of vast sums of money by wealthy politicians and their organizations to use in persuading the voting public to support their cause.

More often than not, that cause seems to result in the election of other unethically minded individuals, or worse, supporting causes that are demonstrably corrupt, dangerous and potentially catastrophic to the best interests of a nation.

19 Politics Without Money

And we all know that money can buy support for special interest groups when often that support is designed to allow those elected to vote and manipulate public sentiment to run counter to the public good.

It is well known that those who already have much more money than they need for optimum lifestyles can very easily manipulate their investments to provide a continuous stream of increasing profit that has virtually no legal limitation.

Hoarding of wealth contributes to a never ending spiral that takes money out of the economy and contributes to a severe imbalance in the means of fair exchange.

An obvious case in point involves the executives of big oil and other fossil fuel giants whose relentless operations maximize their profits while running roughshod over the good sense of the masses who really want clean energy.

Most everyone knows that protecting the environment from irreparable harm due to the ill effects of pollution on health and general well-being are of highest priority.

And many of good sense realize that clean air and water are not worth sacrificing for the sole purpose of enriching the coiffeurs of corporate executives, accounts of wealthy bankers or giving carte blanche to the influence peddling of corrupt politicians to control voters unethically.

The idea that politics can be operational without the use of money has been considered nothing but an impossible dream by most anyone applying their common sense logic.

The goal of limiting money to level the playing field in politics is sought by many progressives, and is considered something that must happen before the logjam of gridlock in Congress and other dictatorial regimes of government can ever be reigned in to accomplish their assigned tasks.

The bitter truth is that the system of allowing money to accumulate in the hands of politicians to buy not only the votes to decide who get elected to office, but also the power to influence the decisions they make for public policy that ends up with the will of the people being entirely ignored either by default or by deliberate actions.

These same policies of money in politics allowed by the system result in the inevitable result that the people in power can force their own ideas into the system and set up clever legalities to make things difficult to change or undo.

These ideas based upon religious ideology and simple greed for more money, power and control over others tend to disallow most beneficial changes whether or not their governing policies are carrying out the will of the people.

Having a corrupt base of elected officials with inordinate amounts of money to their name along with many easy ways to keep adding to their accounts has put an enormous crimp on social justice, and has created a seemingly unstoppable way that the average citizen can do much to bring necessary changes and reform in a reasonable length of time.

Clearly the system of big money in politics has to be replaced with not just a money-reduction system but a true bona-fide money-free experience where monetary influence is disallowed and the energy of politics puts an emphasis on the original premise of the birth of the Republic in 1776.

That premise was that the new government would be kept secure from takeover by special interests that could run counter to what the average citizen really wants and expects from their elected officials.

It is well known that the original purpose of politics in deciding who speaks for the people has pretty much been brushed aside in many governments at all levels because of unethical legalities that have allowed money to determine who is elected and what policies will prevail.

Once money and monetary influence as we know it is removed from the political equation however, the stance of candidates and their ideas can then focus on the question of who is presenting the winning argument for policies that the majority of citizens want for the common good.

19 Politics Without Money

The ShareFlow ECU Network that has been presented in this writing may be the foundation and essentially the only means for effectively eliminating all money and financial influence from the political game.

By design it would allow a more efficient management team to sustain the economic health and social justice that the average citizen demands.

The ShareFlow ECU network would be a system that can potentially do what all other economic systems have failed to do as a result of money-driven gridlock.

Consider how politicians getting paid only in earned credit units would be obliged to perform in a cooperative manner to build mutual trust and avoid conflict and gridlock over ideologies in order to retain their job especially if laws were in place to keep them honest and trustworthy.

Consider how candidates for public office would be selected and eventually filtered out to become the winners in elections under the ShareFlow system.

The first step would be to have each pre-qualified candidate become an 'employee' of a government facility specifically set up to 'hire' all eligible candidates.

By virtue of their eligibility as responsible employees, they are each issued appropriate numbers of earned credit units to cover personal costs and campaign expenses.

Each allotment would have the important stipulation that each candidate for any specified office is allowed only an equal and appropriate number of credit units to be spent for campaign purposes, with no credit units coming in for use from any other source.

This stipulation would put all competing candidates at every level vying for public office on an equal playing field so that no one has a monetary advantage over anyone else.

For all elected officials in Congress and similar legislative branches of government, there would no longer be money for lobbyists to influence voting.

166

19 Politics Without Money

Each elected official would be paid only their qualified number of credit units by virtue of their value as an elected official, with no opportunity to amass unearned wealth.

Every politician no matter what office they held or at what level they perform at would be held accountable for supporting the wishes of the majority of their constituents with the understanding that they would be immediately relieved of office if they were found unreliable.

I suggest an amendment to the Constitution that would allow more than two parties to hold seats in Congress, with rules that would disallow any party to impede any passage of responsible legislation or try to force their will and policies upon any of the others.

Each responsible group of citizens would know that they have representation in a party of their choice according to their numbers to guarantee that their voice will be heard and responsibly considered in every relevant issue.

With earned credit units used in the global economy instead of money for everyone including the President, the Congress and the Supreme Court, the idea of responsible government at every level would be defined in a more logical manner whether it be at a national, state or local level.

With earned credit units issued to every office holder by virtue of their employment alone, the concept of responsible government would have a much better chance of becoming a true reality for all the citizens of any nation.

~20~
Cooperative Competition

Historically speaking, the idea of competition has been firmly rooted in governments and cultural groups associated with certain ideologies that favor the adage that says 'May the better man win', 'It's every man for himself' or 'To the victor goes the spoils'.

A firmly established capitalistic government that resists all attempts to instill policies that reflect anything that looks like 'socialism' in operative nature is the prime example for such deeply rooted ideologies.

Easily accepted is the assumption that it is moral and ethically OK to discourage cooperation that would benefit everyone by producing better products and services to instill a very different type of competition.

Indeed, virtually all capitalistic systems have chosen the type of competition that tends to benefit only the wealthy by making it easy to generate more wealth from profit for them since in their way of thinking, the end justifies the means.

Abundance is supposed to be everyone's right in a fully cooperative economy, but wealthy capitalists tend to support the myth that everyone will benefit when there is hard core competition, since wealth 'creates jobs and money eventually trickles down to everyone else in due time', (yeah, right).

It's a perverse attitude that makes it almost impossible to give any comprehensive help to support the less fortunate who for various reasons do not have the right opportunities to generate a satisfactory life style on their own.

When the top 1% focus all their thoughts on preserving their status quo of wealth and conservatism even when logic dictates that their purse strings need to be loosened in order to benefit everyone which would logically include even themselves, there seems to be no one capable of giving them the education they need but would reject anyway; and by doing so would be an arrogant rebuke to rational thinking.

The conventional wisdom of economic competition has been based upon two driving forces that seem like powerful incentives for customers to take advantage of:

1. If you produce a better product or service than your competitors at a similar cost, you can count on more sales and thus greater profit for yourself over time, and

2. If you offer your product or service of basically equal quality to the public at a lower cost than your competitors, it often results in greater success in selling what you have for more personal profit in the long run.

In the history of doing business in any economy, as long as competition remained a friendly game, everyone would prosper to make a reasonable profit, even as the quality of goods and services tended to gradually improve over time due to better technology for the benefit of everyone.

But now we can clearly see what has happened to the capitalistic system of what was originally considered the only efficient way of producing and distributing many products and services in the United States.

Slowly but surely, wealthy bankers, brokers and CEOs of large corporations began taking over large portions of the money supply that was originally supposed to flow freely into the hands of all citizen regardless of wealth status.

In the everyday world of transactions in commerce and industry, the system should have allowed a more equitable distribution for those purposes no matter what economic class, professional status, or ethnic background the average citizen came from.

Many of us now see that the supposedly efficient and benevolent system of capitalism has actually turned into a quiet nightmare of corrupt proportions that allows unbridled greed, fraud and control of others to flourish at all levels, and continues to go unrestricted by laws or effective legal action that should have been implemented from the very start of the nation's birth in 1776.

Capitalistic competitiveness has resulted in forcing many of the well-deserving citizens and their families into a life of undeserved poverty while the affluent are given a free pass and allowed a continuous and expanding reign to accrue essentially endless amounts of money.

Much of the money the excessively wealthy acquire is taken out of circulation and used for power to control the economy and force others who are disadvantaged out of fair opportunities for quality and equitable living standards.

Obviously the competitive capitalistic system in America is not a well planned and designed way that works for all the common good in terms of producing and distributing the basics necessary to keep everyone adequately supplied.

And just as obviously, the capitalistic system has been damaged by the periodic slow down of recessions and the imbalance of boom and bust eras that routinely create headaches for the average family while trying to create and maintain a sustainable living standard.

Allowing an uncontrolled system based upon supply and demand using competition for money accrual to determine who survives economically has been the game from day one.

When it first began, the game was expected to not only provide abundance in necessary products and services, but create good health and peace of mind free from unnecessary stress... for the winners in the game.

Unfortunately it has not happened for the majority of average citizens and their families who turn out to be the losers as a result of unfair advantages stacked against them from the start that allow only a favored few to be the easy winners in the money-driven capitalistic experience.

The competition began with the idea that anyone could succeed if only they would work real hard at whatever they were doing so that they could produce not only a plethora of great products and services for the masses, but even more importantly - great profit for the managers.

The ongoing myth was supposed to give all of us the enthusiasm for working hard to get ahead while being willing to do our daily tasks in all the various avenues of employment with a sense of great pride in a job well done.

It was supposedly meant to give anyone who followed the rules of hard work, competitiveness and loyalty as a team player a sense of great pride and accomplishment that they achieved company goals with the feeling that everyone was valued and respected no matter what position they held.

Unfortunately what was left out of the equation was the 'equally valued and respected' part.

In its place began the firmly rooted concept that no one could be trusted to do their part, and consequently there had to be the overlords put into place to firmly and decisively (and in many cases quite arrogantly) control the lives of the workers through micromanagement policies.

Micromanagers ignored the foundations of trust, equal value and cooperation in favor of assuring their money and power was secured by perpetual increase in company profit.

The true intent of cooperation in the work force seemed never to be noticeably promoted by any government official, the media, business or corporate management in a manner that would make the idea a powerful force in practice.

Commonly brushed aside now is the realization that the 'me first attitude' so rampant in the destructive competition of capitalism dominating America's economy and in other money systems throughout the global environment could actually be negated and overruled.

Setting our sights too low for achieving change results in ineffective band-aid responses which can create a fallacy of letting buzz-word labels like socialism and liberalism become runaway misunderstandings with the inability to recognize what civilized society really needs.

20 Cooperative Competition

Consider now what can happen once the earned credit unit network is implemented so that money is no longer the object of one's affections.

Consider what can and will happen once money as we know it is eliminated from the global economy and replaced by earned credits called **yuna** issued directly to all those who are gainfully employed in activities that benefit society in general and uphold the common good for all citizens.

What will be recognized as the wave of the future is the realization that opportunities for a sustainable quality of life where everyone benefits can easily become the new norm.

These dreams are not as far-fetched as many would first imagine, since the concept of moneyfree is easily attainable once the system is set up to where everyone is motivated to focus their time, energy and purpose for living to include significant contributions to the common good.

Putting a fair share of effort into the goal of sustaining a free flow of basic products and services for the well-being of society in general would be achieved and be sustainable.

By virtue of well chosen occupations matched to one's skills, personality, experience and interests, it would set up a premise that would alter the economic equation to the betterment of all - based upon mutual trust and cooperation.

With the ShareFlow ECU network in operation, the new system would allow any preferred profession to be available for selection to further one's personal goals.

In doing so, it must also be conducive for creating useful contributions to help improve the standard of living for everyone else in civilized society at large.

For personal benefit, ShareFlow would allow the use of cooperative competition to increase one's earned credit unit wages by producing better products or services so that all workers could benefit their lifestyle without resorting to aggressive tactics that are based upon money and profit.

The result of destructive competition in suppressive dictatorial regimes has been systematic removal of money from the life blood of the economy at every level just like a blood clot stops the flow of life blood to a living organism and threatens death to the system it is supposed to feed.

A ShareFlow ECU network would automatically negate destructive competition for acquiring and hoarding money that has been notoriously used for unnecessary acquisitions of wealth and control of others.

It would also put a halt to the diminishing of natural resources, political corruption, and systematic disruption and destruction of the global environment.

Once the network is in operation, it would operate in a way that allows only beneficial, friendly and cooperative competition that is no longer dependent upon money.

It would be set up for the purpose of providing better products, goods and services that by default should be the real goal of the providers, so that all providers and their recipients benefit in a friendly competitive manner.

~21~
Exponential Efficiency

It seems logical that when we think more rationally about the true purpose of money and the accountability of money, many good things can transpire.

Once the effects of change begin to take place, the increase in awareness of the benefits should bring in more of an 'in vogue' presence among rational thinkers since they can compare the advantages against the alternatives.

The only real use of money was originally intended as a convenient means of maintaining simple accountability for value exchange in any transaction involving goods and services while creating and sustaining a continuous flow of currency as a means to support a healthy economy.

The inventors of money probably never intended it to be used in a way to control and manipulate individuals, groups or nations by having it unjustly constrain and stress citizens with unethical threats of repercussions.

If there was an effective way to teach the world that money itself is not an absolute requirement for an efficient economy and that strict accountability in paying bills is actually an unnecessary drag on quality of life, we would be doing the global community a huge favor and end up with an exponentially efficient way of doing business.

If we could teach just a small segment of the population how sensible it is to eliminate the strict accountability of keeping accounts above zero all the time while making a case that money itself is not all that important, we are on our way to opening the door for an evolution of exponential proportions and at levels never seen before.

21 Exponential Efficiency

Isn't it time to admit that we would all benefit in a profoundly efficient way by working together to adhere to personal responsibility in keeping all necessary goods and services flowing in a more efficient and benevolent cycle?

And couldn't an economic cycle operate without the unnecessary step of having to account for every exchange of value involving the things of obvious importance such as products and services we inherently need for our health, our subsistence and a basic pursuit of our dreams?

I believe we can do this without the negative thinking that is automatically brought forth at every hint that seems to cement the myth that money is an absolute necessity of a civilized society. Hint: It decisively… is not the case!

The exponential benefit to everyone in a truly money-free economic experience is likely to outweigh the mindset of monetary accountability that has held us all in financial slavery since time immemorial.

Why have the benefits not arrived?

Could it be based upon the fear that 'others' would always take advantage of free exchange and not do their part to produce a fair share of products and services without the threat of dire consequences in strict retaliation for non-payment of bills?.

Isn't it time to move on to a more sensible method of running an economy free of stress over adequate income?

I think it is and can be achieved in a step-wise fashion.

Proper education can do a lot to change our thinking when educators are open-minded, seriously consider the concept, and study the plethora of information pertinent to understanding how a moneyfree economy can operate.

Significant benefits can apply even to the wealthy elite and the politicians who think they must 'have it all' right away without giving up any excess wealth or the means to keep it coming regardless of their contributory value to the common good.

Indeed, logical minds are beginning to open up to a concept that involves 'an exponential benefit to all' that can far outweigh the myth that 'too many others would act unfairly and not cooperate to make it work'.

Let us take note of some of the results we can expect when there is no need of strict accountability of money transactions anywhere on the planet!

1. Virtually everyone could gravitate to a profession where they could easily find employment and work in an essentially stress-free environment that would be able to offer reasonable responsibilities free of micromanagement.

2. All workers would be able to perform their duties without the least concern for getting paid because workers would have no bills to pay yet would still obtain all their reasonable necessities by auto-payment with credit units.

This becomes possible when money is removed from the equation of financial operations and eventually phased out completely in favor of earned credit units that could not be transferred to anyone else who did not earn them.

3. Conservatives in governments would no longer be able to withhold funds from anything decisively shown to benefit the common good since their weapon of holding back on funds to rail against socialism in favor of divisive rule would no longer exist.

The so-called national 'debt' would disappear instantly as would all other so-called debt since the concept of debt on a national scale would become meaningless when the accountability for payment of bills no longer exists.

4. There would be no money to fund wars or to pay dictatorial government leaders any assistance to prepare for war because the incentive for supporting conflict would be eliminated at their source.

5. Big Oil and all other fossil fuel developers could no longer buy off renewable clean energy alternatives because there would be no money to buy them off and would leave entrepreneurs virtually free to develop and hire qualified

professionals to mass produce and distribute a wide variety of renewable clean energy systems anywhere and everywhere where it is logical and feasible to do so.

6. Many categories of crime and related activity of an unethical nature would be greatly reduced because the major incentive for crime is to get unlawful acquisition of money that that would harm others and create imbalance to the efficient flow of money in the economy.

7. Every citizen could get healthcare without worrying about needing money to pay for it because the new system of credit units would work to provide universal coverage without accountability for monetary transactions.

8. The Federal Reserve and Internal Revenue Service would end since their purpose would no longer be needed.

9. All the subsistence basics of life including food, clothing and shelter would be made available for everyone without charge because all of these fundamentals would be set up for automatic distribution to all without the usual stress or concern involved in thinking about who is going to pay for it.

10. Accountability to directly pay for anything would end, meaning everyone could live in adequate housing as determined by their employment status and subsequent contributions to the common good.

11. Public utilities could no longer be shut off because of non-payment of bills since bills would no longer exist.

12. Home foreclosures would be non-existent because accountability of payments would not be an issue.

13. Homelessness would end since there would always be a home available for anyone who needs it and is willing to be responsible for the upkeep and maintenance with a commitment to contribute to the welfare of others and the common good in any way they are capable to do so.

14. Politicians would be chosen for their ethics and statesmanship, and not for 'how much money they could raise to manipulate elections or promote their ideologies.

15. Food could be grown locally and affordably for all localities using greenhouse growing without unnecessary concern about the cost of their purchases.

Production and distribution of necessary infrastructure and resources would now be accomplished easily through enhanced production capabilities of modern technology.

16. Mass production of water fueled and electric cars could replace all gas guzzling vehicles because initial costs and expenses normally associated with purchasing any new technology would not exist.

17. Zero point energy technology will eventually phase out all other energy dependencies; most notably including oil, coal, natural gas and nuclear power plants, since ZPE has the potential to be the ultimate renewable clean energy resource to replace everything else.

18. Ocean water could be desalinized as necessary to supply all drought-stricken areas without concern over the cost, since money limitations would no longer exist and the work to accomplish this globally would be provided by employees compensated with their earned credit units by virtue of their employment not tied to profit or costs of resources and equipment.

19. A whole slew of useless occupations would quickly disappear including high-priced attorneys, high paid rock stars, high-end contracts in the world of sports, patent issuing and tracking, copyrighting accountability, banking, credit card companies, currency production, tax collectors, the stock market, investment brokers, financial advisors, debt collectors, gaming and insurance companies, etc..

20. Foreign aid would consist only of men and women working on a volunteer basis to perform useful work, and would no longer include money allocations.

21. Most people would eventually gravitate to the job of their interest, skills, work experience, occupation and profession best suited for their needs and personality.

22. All air, water, ground and food pollution including GMO farming would effectively terminate due to the end of fossil fuel dependency that has stressed and harmed the global population in so many seen and unforeseen ways.

As a result of all this and more, economic efficiency for the common good of society could skyrocket and tend to constantly improve over time instead of getting worse as it always tends to do in our globally stressed money-dependent methodology.

The forgoing examples are just for starters and just the miniscule tip of an iceberg representing the many benefits that our world society would likely see happen once we adjust our thinking to realize that money is not an essential to create and distribute abundance to everyone.

All personal and business accounts in existence would be part of the ECU network with a sophisticated security system to see that only the proper number of credit units go to those qualified by their employment status.

Transactions would take place only between qualified accounts where specified amounts of earned credit units are issued monthly as wages quantified by virtue of the owner's employment status to be spent only for goods and services priced according to value given for value received.

All earned credit units would be issued and activated by ShareFlow, and be available only for payment of wages and spending on products and services.

Once spent, they are deactivated and put in qualified business accounts that confirm they were used to pay for customers' purchases of goods or services.

ShareFlow would evaluate all businesses for inactive units and then discards them since they have done their job by being spent for value received and value earned.

There would be no need to have a total count in ShareFlow of all inactive units coming back to the banking system since it would have an infinite ocean of units to draw from for issuing qualified numbers to each employee thereby keeping an efficient and proper flow of **yuna** units moving throughout the economy.

Wages for every occupation, profession and status of employment would be issued with a certain built in excess to allow for each account holder to accrue a reasonable savings that is not allowed to go over an upper limit cap.

Every dispensation would be based upon calculations considering what is normal for one's specific employment qualification, with the addition of a qualified percentage to maintain a savings account that can go up to but not over a maximum to prevent hoarding or the development of another gap between the wealthy and the poor.

Identity theft would be virtually impossible to establish since all accounts would be managed under the ShareFlow banking system that would automatically flag any attempt to transfer earned credit units to an unqualified account.

Careful planning of the earned credit unit network under ShareFlow would insure that adequate safeguards are tested and put in place to identify every participant in any salary, wage or spending transaction and thus be traceable to a real person in every transaction.

Let's take a look at how overall efficiency compares between our traditional money-driven economies and how a well-designed earned credit unit system would operate by reviewing how credit units (**yuna**) could easily simplify all economic transactions.

When entering a grocery or general merchandise store, we would see that every item would be clearly marked in terms of whole numbers of **yuna** stating the total cost, with no sales tax or signs to mark anything on sale..

Stores would no longer spend money on advertising, issuing coupons, lowering prices for quick sales, or accept any form of traditional money.

That alone would make it easier and quicker for the average customer to shop without spending their time and energy on monetary concerns.

At the check stand, all items would be added up for total cost so that customers could use their debit cards to pay for their items by withdrawing the appropriate number of **yuna** from their personal accounts in ShareFlow.

These earned credit units having been spent are put into inactive status in the store's business account that also resides in ShareFlow so that these specific units can never be spent again or transferred for any other purpose.

ShareFlow would keep track of all spent **yuna** coming in from total sales over time to confirm how well each store is doing business.

That information is audited and used to maintain each store's status as a successful entity to continue to employ their required number of employees.

For the benefit of every store and their customers, the efficiency of operation may increase over time so that the cost of business could go down to allow the inclusion of free of charge items whenever there would be an excess of specific merchandise in stock.

As the number of free items offered by any business grows over time, this practice alone enables a slow but sure trend of strengthening the moneyfree concept while at the same time weakening the traditional requirement of strict monetary accountability for all transactions.

As long as each employee of any business maintains an acceptable history of reasonable performance, his or her status remains qualified for a specific salary and noted as such in the company's monthly report to ShareFlow.

For all business operations from large corporations to small businesses including sole proprietorships, the idea is basically the same, so that no matter how large or small a business is, their basic accounting duties are similar.

Accounting duties would simply include keeping track of how many qualified workers are employed, how many **yuna** are to be paid in salary for each job description, and the monthly reports to ShareFlow on how the business is doing in terms of total earned credit units already spent by customers for purchase of products or services normally offered by the business.

Even the accounting duties of governments could be handled in similar fashion, since a government would also be considered a business without the stigma of traditional fraud associated with out-of-control issues over money.

Government accounts would have to be constrained and obliged to follow the same rules of accounting as any other business by dealing with **yuna** for wages issued to all their employees including the President, Congress and the Supreme Court, etc.

In a successful global economy, all governments would need to provide strict accountability to the ShareFlow ECU network operating as the only banking system in existence, being universal, properly authorized and managed, and always totally transparent to every citizen to assure that proper safeguards are always maintained to protect every account holder.

The U.S. Congress would be constrained to pass laws that support and maintain every qualified social program including equivalences of adequate universal healthcare, social security, adequate education for all levels, renewable clean energy development, protection of the environment, and acceptable aid to other countries.

Pulling unauthorized money out of the air to support military and war efforts could no longer happen, since all funding would be controlled by the only banking system in existence called ShareFlow using earned credit units in lieu of anything to do with traditional money accountabilities.

In spite of being the only banking system in existence, it could still be totally transparent to all citizens and thus allowed to issue whatever earned credit units are needed to maintain qualified transactions from an infinite ocean of **yuna** where the term monetary debt no longer applies.

21 Exponential Efficiency

All vehicle purchases such as cars and trucks would be on a sensible leasing plan so that customers' time of usage, cost of maintenance and repairs or replacement as needed would be accounted for by allowing a monthly debit from their personal accounts with no interest or debt accrued.

For purchasing a home or similar big ticket item, the sale could also be handled by leasing using debits of **yuna** as monthly payments instead of having outright purchase ownership from the start.

In each case it would make good sense in terms of efficiency and usage that all such items should be time related regarding their usage and change in value.

To bottom-line the concept of exponential efficiency in an earned credit unit economy, there would likely be a rapid increase in the sense of freedom for all citizens when they finally realize how so many time consuming complications of traditional monetary accountability had forced so many of them into essentially useless occupations.

Indeed it is now abundantly clear that many are driven out of necessity to support a system of complex monetary manipulations instead of having opportunities to do things they would rather be doing that bring joy to the soul but not profit to the excessively wealthy.

~22~
Setting the Priorities

The word *priority* is a term that would always demand a definition relative to a point of reference depending upon how inclusive the word is intended for use.

Logically in this context, *priorities* should be defined something like 'relative to the common good, health and well-being of a nation's economy or society in general'.

This can include such things as all the basics needed for a reasonable quality of life, plus the means to maintain the health of the environment.

For the imperfect society we live in, the definition would have to include a certain degree of support for the military and a police force that could systematically be reduced over time as nations and ultimately the entire global community eventually learns to work together for the benefit of all.

Considering the top priorities for society's needs that result in higher quality of life without the fear factors of demanding unlimited funds for police and military, we can consider priorities that provide for the common good with funding for sensible and qualified social programs.

These are the priorities of many who want to help those in true need by not resorting to obsessive concerns over security issues that keep planning for a never ending defense against real and perceived terrorists at home and abroad.

Let us consider some of the many services of modern living that have changed our life style over the years and can now be considered high priority for an efficient economy.

Examples should include all the labor and resources needed to provide for health and well-being to minimize the discomfort of sickness, accidents and challenges of nature.

22 Setting The Priorities

Logically it should not include unnecessary products or occupational labor deemed frivolous or antiquated in light of a proposed ShareFlow earned credit unit system.

Conversely, the determination of non-priorities should include discussions about many occupations involving the production or distribution of any product or activity deemed harmful to the common good.

Common sense says that non-priorities in the economy should include such things as illegal drugs, liquor, tobacco, gaming interests, political posturing, influence peddling and payoffs to special interests that cannot be seen as necessary or useful to our well being as a society.

If the ShareFlow network begins with a single nation replacing their currency with an electronic financial network of earned credit distribution centers, there should be a well-planned procedure to determine true social need priorities for adequate support in every state or district equitably.

As an approximation to declaring a general list of the priorities that define quality of life for humans and other life forms on the planet, we can start with a **Tier 1** top priority level to include our obvious dependency on having adequate oxygen, water and food for simple survival.

This implies that the environment must be protected from the onslaught of man-made pollution and destruction of natural resources that secure these basic necessities.

Similarly a **Tier 2** level of priorities could include basic items that define civilized living including adequate clothing, shelter from the elements, vehicles for basic transportation, the normal means of communication and clean energy for commerce, industry and protection from the elements.

This level could logically include public utilities, postal service, and reasonable protection from injuries and loss that the fire departments, police and other emergency service personnel are set up for to protect the citizens.

Tier 2 priorities might also include providing for various levels of information services including radio, television, the internet, the news media, and forms of transportation and public utilities necessary to efficiently support production and distribution of the totality of goods and services that define and maintain a civilized world.

Additional necessities of everyday living would include hospitals, medical clinics, health care services, facilities and service personnel for education and the infrastructures for public use such as walkways, buildings, parks, highways, etc.

Considering the definition of goods and services to be all inclusive for everything money is now used for should include everything deemed reasonable and necessary for the common good of citizens throughout all nations.

A **Tier 3** level might include all professions providing work to support and maintain the higher levels of public education, science, exploration, advanced technologies, and research and development in the various fields of medicine, renewable clean energy and space exploration, etc.

Logically it would also include systems that help protect the ecosystem from natural or man-made threats that could potentially harm the global environment.

With the ShareFlow ECU network in operation, money limitations would no longer be the overriding issue that has so often stopped adequate funding for social programs that benefit the common good since in these cases, money would no longer exist.

Thankfully it would be replaced by non-transferrable earned credit units that every qualified worker and employee would be guaranteed by virtue of their employment.

For the ShareFlow system of credit units to be allocated according to how an occupational description is defined would require a well-thought-out analysis to identify and include all the tier variables as part of the equation.

For example, an occupation that involved a significant degree of environmental protection for air, water or food production could certainly be rated more valuable in terms of how many earned credit units should be earned by a worker in one of those occupations as compared to how many that same person should earn by simply being in the business of making a better widget than one's neighboring business can do.

In short, to begin the process of setting the priorities of what goods and services should be included in priority fashion for the ECU System, we would first eliminate all support for occupational descriptions that either harm or in no logical way are considered useful for society in general.

Then we could allocate the number of credits for each job description according to the overlying principal of 'value received for value given' and be rated relative to how well it contributes to the over-all benefit of the common good.

Since earned credit units would be issued only to those who have a legitimate occupation deemed useful to society, the consideration of priorities should pertain to not only the credits an individual can receive by reason of employment, but also to what those credit units are qualified to be used for in terms of purchasing products and services.

Regarding what occupations should be qualified for the ECU network and what types of work should not qualify would evolve in such a manner that would encourage the consideration of switching occupations when necessary.

Changing one's profession should not only reflect one's preferences and interests, but also be in line with priorities defined by computer analysis that determine the quantified numbers of credits for each job description.

The ECU network planning stages could provide the natural selection process of qualified occupations for young people to consider so that many could gravitate toward an education that best suits their interests and talents geared to their choice of priorities.

The variables would include not only their personal interests, education and work history skills, but also the occupational descriptions that are in line with employment rated at the highest priority levels to allow greater earned credit unit payment in wages and salaries.

The natural selection process of career choices would then slowly weed out the desire for occupations that do not provide great benefit to individuals or society in general, and would tend to phase out anyway by attrition over time.

Natural selection would encourage employees in certain occupations to gravitate to more desirable forms of work that would force businesses and job descriptions of lesser value to be eliminated when demands for their goods or services phase out over time.

Examples of businesses that would tend to fade away or reduce operations might be liquor companies, tobacco firms, bar tending, attorneys, courtroom personnel, certain high-priced sport stars and casino operations.

Also included would be the proliferation of advertising agencies, charity organizations, credit card companies, loan companies, competitive bankers, and a host of occupations in the fossil fuel industries including oil, gas, and coal.

Once infrastructure equipment and maintenance items are manufactured more reliably and efficiently due to the abundant availability of clean renewable energy, the need for system inspectors will likely diminish over time.

The talk of robots taking jobs away from fearful workers who understandably have worries over loss of income will ultimately become a good thing in that many jobs involving stressful labor will disappear, and the income of the workers will not be substantially affected due to other opportunities of immediate employment elsewhere.

The good news of course would be that any displaced worker would instantly have a greater selection of enjoyable and healthful professions and alternatives to choose from.

All high priority occupations delivering the most useful work to society would begin to eliminate the least useful labor to the benefit of all businesses and employees so that workers would no longer have to worry about loss of jobs.

22 Setting The Priorities

A reasonable question to ask at this point is who would actually make the decisions regarding the priority levels of all definable occupations in order to maximize cooperation and minimize disagreements about which professions are most important and which may not even be necessary or should be set at a lower priority to qualify for compensation.

Online input using a hack-proof internet system from the people of each nation would be a logical way to decide the priority schedule of all occupations that could be set up for priority voting to determine the hierarchy that would qualify each work description accordingly.

Online priority voting for every locality could be set up to qualify each job description accordingly so that selected priorities would properly reflect the opinions of the majority of voters on the importance of each job description.

They could vote on how valuable each work description contributes to the common good so that a proper number of earned credit units could be quantified in accordance with their perceived hierarchy of priorities.

To respond to changes over time, future online input could be relied upon in the above manner to fine tune the priorities to reflect changing conditions regarding how jobs should be rated and might need to be given greater or lesser compensation than others.

Let's consider a scenario of businesses that would likely exist in a dynamic ShareFlow ECU network based system using earned credit units instead of money.

Solar and wind energy conversion systems would already be in full operation as the main source of energy resources for the nation, but promising entrepreneurs might bring out new technologies that use zero point energy systems that would be more efficient, adaptable and maintained easily due to small unit size and portability for almost any location.

Let's say that a new company called Space Wave Energy Systems is created that announces many new openings for employment to design, fabricate, distribute and demonstrate the capabilities of a promising new line of renewable clean energy products for home and industry.

Let's say SWES offers openings for engineers, computer programmers, scientists and technicians to develop and support a variety of essentially portable box systems that produce electricity in various power ratings from small light portable usage to home energy systems on up to a variety of heavy industrial requirements.

Many of these job openings would offer on-the-job-training for basically qualified personnel previously hired to the solar and wind conversion industries.

In this example,, Space Wave Energy Systems would be set up to offer even greater efficiencies in clean energy usage including the mass production and portability of zero point energy products to make them applicable for a wider range of locations globally.

Once the advantages are well advertised, online input from citizens would likely favor prioritizing the zero point conversion products as compared to solar and wind systems as being more versatile and efficient for general use.

ZPE systems would likely garner greater support and offer greater credit unit compensation to workers at Space Wave Energy Systems than other companies world-wide that did not use zero point conversion as the source for their clean energy product development.

For a less dramatic example of change in employment, let's consider companies that now use 3-D copiers or even robots to fabricate products that previously had to be put together manually by workers on an automated assembly line (a common cause for job disappearance nowadays).

Not to worry, because in a ShareFlow ECU economy, there would be many opportunities for all displaced workers to instantly phase into a variety of new or related industries, many of which would likely offer on-the-job-training and even greater benefits than prior employers had previously been willing to offer.

22 Setting The Priorities

No matter what industry or business is phased out or is deemed unnecessary for the welfare of the common good, there would be more than enough opportunities for instant income replacements along with new job assignments made available for all displaced workers.

In virtually all cases, workers who lose their jobs would suffer no setback when they gravitate or become assigned to more efficient and desirable work in industries that have a high priority of occupations available for the good of society as determined by citizen input online.

Labor unions would no longer be necessary, and the personnel involved in industries such as competing credit card and loan companies would no longer be employed in work focusing on profit and money manipulation alone.

The ShareFlow employment priority system would then morph into a self-corrective manner of operation that would always be readily transparent to the general public and be available for cooperative fine tuning by citizen input as a standard of maintaining efficiency and stress-free living in a global economy that works for all its citizens.

~23~
Bartering for Equal Value

When the subjects of barter and trade come up, one might thoughtfully ask if it is really necessary that every value for value exchange in life has to be handled with either the exchange of money or the use of earned credit units.

Obviously many transactions can occur without money or even credit units being involved in an exchange of goods or services between any two or more individuals, or between businesses for necessary acquisitions using the philosophy of 'value given for value received'.

Even with a system that goes totally moneyfree at some point, there will likely be many situations where neither money nor earned credit units would be practical, feasible, necessary or even possible, especially for matters deemed frivolous or conveniently handled with a trade agreement.

The related concepts of barter, trade and gift giving have existed since the dawn of human existence and are certainly useful methods of dealing with exchanges of products and services on a level where presumed accountability of value is not strictly necessary.

Many common examples can be pointed out such as home grown fruits or vegetables being traded for different fruits and vegetables or related items such as garden tools, soil amendments, lawn mowing, snow shoveling, etc.

Such considerations as these involving exchanges for alternative commodities using approximation for equal value can be easily determined and should be more than adequate to uphold the spirit and philosophy of value comparison.

The concepts of barter and trade can be considered as equivalent terminology in our times because it is not just individuals or families involved when products and services are exchanged with the approximation of satisfying 'value given for value received'.

The concept of trade has involved nations, corporations, states and other business entities whenever there is any type of exchange of products and services desired.

Commodity trading can be a useful practice whenever the alternative of money exchanging hands is not always the best way or even necessary while keeping value transactions defined as fair exchange.

The use of barter is obviously useful when there is no formal business arrangement involving individuals or if there is no substantial difference defined in a theoretical 'value given for value received' transaction.

Agreement to use barter and trade can be set up without the calculation of strict monetary equivalence in goods and services whenever there are products or resources on both sides of the exchange that are mutually considered of high priority without strict dollar for dollar accountability.

Gift giving of course is another area for consideration because the giving of gifts does not expect a tangible return of value whenever used by one party who wants to donate something to another in exchange for intangible benefits.

The intangibles that a gift giver experiences receiving from the recipient over time usually includes such things as love, respect, compassion, support, empathy or promise of cooperation in future transactions.

Strictly speaking, the act of gift giving has not fallen into the broad definition of barter or trade, but the concept can be interpreted as such when there are intangibles involved.

It is well known that gift giving is normally an act that allows for no tangible value to be expected in return.

This is simply a reminder that some things in life do not need strict accountability for 'value given for value received' and can be considered the exceptions to the expectations of accountability in monetary value exchange.

23 Bartering for Equal Value

When considering previous chapters on specifying what goods and services should be defined as being of subsistence needs for free distribution to everyone regardless of their employment status, 'barter' takes on an enhanced meaning.

Although free of charge, each gift of subsistence can be turned into a barter or trade situation by simply asking the needy person (such as a homeless man for example) to offer and perform some simple community service.

By offering a simple service to the local community in exchange for a gift of subsistence, it becomes a barter of sorts to encourage him learn greater responsibility for taking charge of his own welfare and by doing so gain an incentive to gravitate to an occupation and a new situation that can lift him out of his state of homelessness.

Talking about barter, trade and gift giving may seem insignificant compared to an automated credit unit network that can pay any man, woman or child a compensation for anything of value in return for labor or service performed; however the benefit of bringing in a new sense of worth to many folks who have felt down and out or in some manner 'worthless' has the potential to turn their life around.

When one stops to think more carefully about the use of barter and trade, their significance will likely take on greater enhancement as the related concept of money accountability and dealing with money to pay bills gradually disappears from the stage of everyday living.

With the global ECU network replacing the need for any monetary exchange for value received according to value earned, the reality of trade between nations can take on an expanded role with the potential of large scale operations never before seen or even thought possible.

Consider for example a third world country lacking the resources, conveniences and efficient means for sustaining even the basics of life for the majority of their citizens.

Unfortunately at the time of this writing, such examples are quite common in the Middle East and Africa, and as most everyone knows, it results in disastrous consequences for large segments of the world's population.

Instead of unparalleled sums of money being allocated to support military operations around the world, there could be new policies of helping other nations take on the role of being more self-supportive through self-help by the citizens.

Teaching other nations to be self-supportive can bring them back and more in line with the economically privileged nations such as the United States and other countries by using barter and trade of commodities and resources that each nation needs and depends upon.

Real economic aid to all third world countries could and would logically become a reality and provide many services in exchange for scarce resources in a manner similar to the Peace Corp operations employing many capable youth of all nations who seek employment and are willing to work in a non-profit atmosphere.

With monetary profit no longer part of the motivation and equation of necessity for the leaders of impoverished nations, resources, products and services can be transferred through barter and trade to where they are needed the most.

This practice can take place while creating benefits such as education and assistance in construction of infrastructure in the poverty stricken areas in exchange for manpower and acquisition of scarce resources not readily available within the nations offering aid.

And since I am talking about 3rd World countries in this context, the question naturally arises as to what can the most poverty stricken nations of the world offer in exchange for foreign aid that the ShareFlow ECU network could set up for credit unit transactions without the use of traditional monetary accountability?

Quite simply, each nation that wants to accept foreign aid of any type would likely have to work out a plan with the countries offering aid that whatever natural resources are available in the impoverished nations will be offered in trade along with manpower, labor and acceptance of education that can ultimately lead to that nation's self-sufficiency and participation in the ECU network by all their citizens.

As the benefits and efficiency of the ShareFlow network become clearly understood and observed in the laboratory of the global environment, any arrangement using barter and trade between nations could be set up in accordance with a planned phase-over to the credit unit network when the time is right so that all parties can appreciate the benefits.

The ShareFlow network would make it much easier to transfer resources, commodities and service personnel as needed when compared to what often happens in a money-driven arrangement, since money and profit considerations often involve bureaucratic complications that could all be avoided when only manpower and credit units are used.

Avoiding potential complications makes it possible for products and services to be delivered directly to the point of need and into the hands of authorized personnel that would provide security for disallowing any criminal elements to interfere with the goals of both sides of the transaction.

Once all nations embrace the idea of dealing with earned credit units via the ECU network, even the concept of barter can take on a more precise meaning by standardizing the values of all products and resources that would normally be available for direct barter or trade without the need for using monetary accountability.

This would be accomplished by assigning values for specific quantities of products in terms of x number of **yuna** credit units per standard quantity of each item.

For a simple example, let us say that Cuba wishes to deal with Brazil by offering a standard quantity of cane sugar in direct trade for a standard quantity of coffee beans so that the barter operation avoids money but each country gets a fair share of the product the other offers in trade.

For that to be successful, let's say that cane sugar is assigned by the ECU network to have a standard value of

2400 **yuna** per ton, and coffee beans are assigned a standard value of 1200 **yuna** per ton available in trade.

In this example, a direct barter operation might simply be agreed upon by both nations so that for every ton of cane sugar Brazil gets from Cuba, Brazil would offer 2 tons of coffee beans to Cuba as a fair trade value of exchange.

If every product and resource (including services given for services received) in direct barter or trade were likewise assigned a standard value in terms of **yuna** credit units, the same philosophy of value given for value received is adhered to each time any nation offers their products, resources or service to another nation in trade.

Standardizing commodities and services for equivalent value would allow many different products to be offered in direct trade to simplify transactions and avoid the monetary accountability of payment of bills, credit complications and other inefficiencies that waste time and energy in the usual money-driven manner.

~24~
Volunteer Workers

Volunteer workers have existed from time immemorial in countless situations that demanded action to accomplish needed tasks where compensation was neither planned for nor expected, but whose tasks were completed out of sheer desire to serve their communities as needed.

Indeed, many people wish to volunteer their energy and time by not being forced to stressfully perform a job simply to keep enough money coming in to pay their bills.

In a perfect world, all work should be performed and rewarded with the philosophy of 'value given for value earned', but much 'value given' by volunteer work is not measurable in terms of equitable compensation.

Even so, the indefinable rewards can be extensive and are often felt by those performing the work as something of real value to themselves and to others with the realization that it may not be compensated monetarily, but still be of real value to those seeing the results in terms of the benefits to the common good delivered to their community.

A simple example are the many volunteers who perform necessary functions at schools and generate many out-of-class learning experiences for children at all levels who can benefit from the teaching moments of those who volunteer their time and energy.

Other examples are those who volunteer their services at senior centers and hospitals such as helping with the many tasks involving the care of the elderly or infirmed, all of which are performed without monetary compensation.

With the advent of a sustained effort to phase out of the money-driven economy in favor of a relatively moneyfree society based upon non-transferable earned credit units, we can assume that some of the folks previously classified as volunteers can now become part of a system of quantifying justifiable compensation.

In fact we could sensibly identify a new profession called professional volunteering using the 'value given for value earned' philosophy that could qualify an appropriate number of earned credit units to issue to everyone with that status.

In other words, volunteers could now be given the same status as anyone else who would have employed status and therefore their status cards for earned credit units would reflect their qualification for an appropriate number of **yuna** earned as a volunteer, and treated as qualified employment.

Having the status as a volunteer worker would give that person a deserved recognition with the understanding that he or she is on call for responding to assignments normally associated with approved work duties that unpaid volunteers would normally accept for their assignments.

In the business world there are many workers known as the 'temps' or temporary help who are trained to step in to a variety of job assignments ranging from the hard labor of construction crews to the skilled office personnel who learn software applications, telephone work, bookkeeping, filing and clerical, etc. that a normal business office requires.

With the ShareFlow ECU network of earned credits in operation to replace money transactions, there would likely be a huge stock of willing workers who could be classified as professional volunteers for periodic assignments and other examples of temporary labor.

This status would have the advantage of operating at the convenience of both management and employed workers so that temporary help of volunteers as professionals would qualify them as being self-employed and have appropriate financial support in the form of earned credit units.

There are many situations where the use of the term 'volunteer' can apply, but in the case of official volunteer status, these workers can be qualified for a certain level of earned credit units in line with their interests, track record and basic skills, with the understanding that they are always available to actually volunteer (choose their assignments) on a reasonably specific basis to perform whatever important assignments are available for them at the time.

Professional volunteer assignments could be prioritized according to what work is available and in line with the jobs one is willing to accept and be best suited for according to each person's time, energy and capabilities.

Even though professional volunteers would be assigned with an on-call status, as long as their status is verifiable and seen as a position of trust in terms of value of work being performed, there is no reason why they should not be given earned credit units as a continuing salary that could now be treated as contributory employment for the betterment of society and the common good.

Professional volunteer work may seem trivial compared to that of others in more noteworthy levels of community service, yet the ECU credit unit system could easily adapt to an on-call status as worthy of payment of earned credit units equitably adjusted and in line with contributory value using the 'value received for value given' philosophy.

Another type of volunteer in the ECU network world would include all those who choose to live without being issued money or earned credits, but simply want to live a simple existence of basic needs and a desire to occasionally lend a hand unofficially in response to their local community needs wherever and whenever they happen to exist and have an opportunity to respond to.

These are the simple-living souls who are basically happy with their existence living close to nature who choose to shun the technologies of civilization but nevertheless have empathy and compassion for their fellowmen.

These are the ones willing to prove it by stepping in for volunteer work whenever they see an opportunity to do so.

And these are the individuals who are willing to perform useful work outside of their normal routine and are happy to live their lives accepting only what they have selected as their basic essentials.

Their subsistence items may be augmented occasionally by coming into town for food, clothing and other items they are not able to self-generate on their own.

The potential for assigning work to these individuals in 3rd world countries is enormous as long as they are all given the choice to either accept a position of work with on-the-job training, work with an official volunteer status, or simply let themselves be available to do whatever type of work they are able and willing to do as needed.

Professional volunteer work can be desirable to many who think of themselves as somewhat of a 'jack-of-all-trades and master of none' type who have the advantage of control over their time to make more choices regarding the number and type of jobs they are willing to accept.

For this status, the number of credit units these folks can qualify for could be set up according to the assignments and type of work they are ready to volunteer for and would need to be in line with their track record of work history, their education and their skills

Other variables for consideration would include added credits for travel expenses, number of dependents who are not already receiving credit units, possible hazardous duty payment and additional credits for special equipment such as needed for responding to forest fires, floods or other natural challenges of nature.

For example as is often the case, many ordinary citizens are called up for hazardous duty from time to time, and in emergency circumstances might be called up to fight a forest fire or a flood and would need extra equipment as a result.

Additional payouts of **yuna** credit units can be allocated as necessary on either a semi-permanent basis or as a one-time payout whenever the duties of a professional volunteer exceed their normal requirements.

Operating within the ShareFlow network; these folks would need to receive extra credit units for several things including hazardous duty status, special equipment for use at the disaster location and compensation for travel expenses to and from the locations where their help as a volunteer is needed very quickly.

A good choice for a jack-of-all-trades type of volunteer would be one where healthy young adults with professional volunteer status are normally stationed in a fixed location such as their home town and can respond to a wide variety of situations involving their skills as temporary workers.

They might respond as temporary help for a large variety of construction or infrastructure maintenance assignments, or in office jobs that routinely require some temporary help to step in when the normal work force may be short of their usual staff of workers.

For example let's assume that Martin O'Connor has made a decision to take up permanent residence in his home town of Terra Haute, Indiana and apply for employment status as a professional volunteer.

Martin is middle aged, married with two children and has had extensive experience with mechanical and electrical maintenance work in his community.

Martin applies to ShareFlow for his new status and is promptly accepted as a professional volunteer for temporary assignment work in his community at large.

Stepping in at his first assignment with a construction company, he works for 5 days in a new housing project and is authorized by the company (Harlow Construction) to be compensated for his labor over that period of time.

ShareFlow verifies his status and confirms that Martin has actually performed the labor, so he is issued his first allotment of earned credit units as a professional volunteer.

A few days later, Martin is hired to repair some minor carpentry in a home that was recently damaged by a violent wind storm and is given authorization by the home owner with a report to ShareFlow that he is on the job to verify his standard credit unit allocation as a result of his assignment.

Even though Martin is not employed by a single entity, his status allows ShareFlow to give him direct compensation for the standard number of credit units he is qualified for as a professional volunteer through client verification that he has performed his assignments as expected.

Many examples like this could be listed in an endless variety of situations, but the point being that often times the compensation for professionally employed volunteers can be set up in a manner consistent with the variability of their work duties according to both the type and quantity of work they perform as determined by the overriding principle of value paid for value earned.

~25~
Controlled Environment Greenhouses

When the subject of professional volunteer work is considered for areas of the economy where one can best find enjoyable work without extensive skills or significant education, certain agriculturally related pursuits are a natural that can easily assimilate many by having them work with food production at the root source (pun intended).

At the time of this writing, the subject of greenhouse growing in our world economy is widely established as an alternate means of contributing to global food production, yet it is not well advertised as a potentially viable source for replacing the extensive farming methods so well established over countless generations.

Many reasons are given as to why intensive greenhouse growing methods have not taken precedence over extensive acreage agriculture, but quite obviously it all comes down to the well-known conservative cliché: 'It costs too much!'

Because our climate is changing to the tune of making extensive farming more and more difficult for many farmers due to climate change events, the idea of going to controlled environment greenhouses CEGs) for our food production is gaining more tenacity by becoming more cost effective even as the business world continues to resist sensible changes that could benefit the entire global population.

The advantages of CEG food production are many, so I list some of the obvious ones in this chapter as a counter to the gridlock thinking that something like this always 'costs too much in up front expenses to set up'.

It is well known that CEGs can be engineered in many different shapes, designs and sizes, and can be set up most anywhere that is practical for sun, adequate water, good soil nutrients and suitable atmospheric growing conditions.

In a money-driven economy, the bottom line of costs always takes precedence over long-term benefits, and the idea that CEGs make good sense in areas where climate is unpredictable is an idea that is often cast aside as a result.

With a globally based ECU Network of earned credits based upon employment instead of employment based upon profit, all food production workers could be successfully employed as agriculturally based workers without stressful monetary concerns.

Food products raised in CEGs are quite often of equal or higher value and quality than their counterpart products grown by traditional extensive farming acreage because of the inherent advantages they can offer over vast acreages.

Being controlled environment based, they can be set up with more optimal growth conditions in terms of sun, water, atmospheric conditions, and soil mixtures customized for the type of produce each CEG is focused on producing.

With renewable clean energy sources operating on the spot or relatively close by, the cost of fossil fuel use is totally eliminated and plant growth is sustainable and can essentially be a 24/7 and 365 days per year operation.

Typically solar energy is directly used by plants and can be a good source for producing electricity during the day, while wind turbines can contribute significantly day or night to keep the power levels sustainable as needed for heating or cooling most any day of the year.

Adequate water can be collected in specially designed collector troughs from rainfall and pumped to each CEG plant layout even where adequate rain is infrequent and not dependable for extensive farming production.

Adequate water can also be obtained by other means including the desalination of ocean water in all locations sufficiently close to sea water sources by relying on pipelines for water distribution rather than for oil transport.

25 Controlled Environment Greenhouses

One obvious advantage of CEGs is that they no longer depend upon the bottom line of cost considerations for long distance distribution and processing required of agricultural products produced by extensive farming.

Local food production and distribution using CEGs is more efficient and generally of better quality due to reduced reliance upon freezing, canning or cooling compared to food that has to be stored and distributed over long distances.

One important factor not talked about significantly to the general public is the nutrient quality of soil preparation for specific crop production that can be easily enhanced in greenhouse growing, and the fact that every plant product raised for food actually requires specific essentials in optimal quantities for growth and food nutrients.

CEGs with their advantage of small space requirements along with easily attached soil preparation rooms can thus guarantee that any crop grown in CEG soil can be supplied with at least adequate soil conditions, and often be given an optimal mix in terms of texture, granular content, moisture retention, water runoff and fertilization value.

When each farmer with a limited acreage to work with purchases at least one CEG with the intention of producing much of the produce required in that locality, he or she can gradually add more CEG modules as required to fulfill the needs of the community over time.

Having a ShareFlow ECU network working for them, farmers could operate without worry of cost, since all costs for installation and maintenance of every greenhouse would be paid for by earned credit units.

Just like any other occupation, earned credit units can be issued to all agriculturally employed workers or professional volunteers as opposed to relying on money and profit to pay salaries that were so contentious in days gone past.

CEGs can be constructed to best suit each locality with specific climate conditions, so that a fairly optimal operation could be set up most anywhere to avoid major disruption.

25 Controlled Environment Greenhouses

The ECU network to stabilize the economy and abolish hunger makes the case for providing high quality produce and certain indoor farm-raised fish that could support many times over a world population that the money-driven profit world does not allow, let alone even wish to consider.

Anyway you wish to look at it; controlled environment greenhouses can offer a host of advantages using intensive growth technologies, skilled and unskilled labor, and the resiliency to adjust to changing conditions that extensive farming methods do not often allow.

What follows here is a summary of the most important advantages CEGs can offer over traditional extensive farms, much of which is proven technology used for generations.

As technology advances, so do the advantages of most life-dependent industries such as our food production and distribution methods in agriculture.

With CEG farming there are major differences inherent with a moneyfree operation compared to our traditional money-driven dependency on profit accountability.

Considering the obvious fact that greenhouse growing has been used successfully for growing a large variety of produce in a small area, consider the advantages of what can be done with that same intensive method used for a large variety of produce as opposed to vast acreage farming.

Many CEGs set up locally over traditional farm acreage can eliminate or reduce the damage of drought or floods, or even disruptions in planting cycles by adjusting the variables in a controlled environment to balance out the disadvantage of a smaller harvest compared to extensive farming.

Even if only one crop is grown in this manner, the advantages of intensive farming are enormous when one considers that a ShareFlow network economy can eliminate the major resistance of upfront costs and maintenance.

There are many possible construction designs suitable for various climate conditions, but the one factor that needs to be common to all is easy maintenance that can be met with modular construction components mass produced and distributed to all localities that have CEGs in operation.

Instead of large unit modular designs, they can be made with smaller mass produced replaceable modules of various designs, and then distributed to all CEG localities as needed for initial construction or stored on the premises for use as storm damage replacement units.

With a ShareFlow ECU network, costs for optimizing growing conditions would no longer be an issue so it would make good sense for all CEG farmers to have special rooms or buildings set aside to prepare and maintain soil conditions that are optimized for specific crops they want to grow.

When there is more than one crop being grown in the same CEG farm layout, it would be logical to have separate rooms for separate soil conditions as necessary or desired to help maximize crop output on a continuous basis.

For crops that are normally grown only in the tropics or semi-tropical climates, it may be more advantageous to bring in native soils from those locations, or arrange for artificially prepared soils that closely meet the natural conditions of the native soil environments once the bio-chemical conditions have been accurately determined.

Carrying that idea one step further, it would be logical to have soil manufacturing companies set up in localities near the sites where initial soil conditions need to be modified as the CEGs are being constructed.

Maintaining optimum soil conditions would increase the efficiency factor for each specialized crop environment after being initially set up with optimized soil content, and could be amended occasionally with soil systematically optimized by the soil manufacturers.

And with the ECU network in operation, fossil fuel use would be totally eliminated in favor of free renewable clean energy from a variety of sources.

If we consider only the first two most widely accepted sources of renewable energy at the time of this writing, we can see how they can work together so efficiently with CEG technology, since solar and wind energy conversion units operate in a semi-complimentary way as supported by nature in a mutually compatible manner.

Solar energy collectors are a natural since the CEGs themselves can be outfitted with collectors of various types adjustable to specific needs, and can be augmented by wind conversion units to take up the slack when there is no sun.

By adding the counterpart of wind energy collectors, we get a highly self-sufficient means for most any locality on Earth to have at least a partial state of independence from fossil fuels that will ultimately phase out completely as public education and efficiency factors steadily improve.

Even if efficiency reaches a perceived plateau of limited value at some point, the cost factor of moving on with CEG development is completely taken out of the equation in an ECU network economy, thus disposing of the major excuse for perennial resistance to the CEG concept.

And once an effective combination of renewable clean energy sources are harnessed and working in tandem for the benefit of the common good, CEG farming can benefit the global economy in a major way since electricity for running all the CEG equipment can be provided at every locality free of the corporate grids.

CEGs are reproducible and can be efficiently maintained so that modular units for all CEG equipment required for sustained operations can be easily produced and delivered anywhere with no cost concerns in an ECU economy.

The use of varied sizes and designs to accommodate specific locations and climate conditions as well as meeting demand for various types of produce would be a good way of getting the general public involved in CEG growing.

It all happens much easier with an ECU network driving the incentives to mass produce everything needed because there would no longer be upfront costs to worry about.

209

25 Controlled Environment Greenhouses

The sheer variety of crops that could be grown in CEGs would seem likely to spark a storm of interest in the whole idea of controlled environment farming everywhere when upfront costs are no longer a factor of significant concern.

Another factor to add to the efficiency and quality of CEG grown produce could be found in the use of extensive rain-water salvage units that would direct certain areas of natural rainfall into storage ponds for use with plants being grown in the area to give them added nutrients normally found in rain as opposed to city water.

With moneyfree methods taking hold in the economy, the resistance efforts of those who complain that rain water is supposed to be left alone to drain into rivers that benefit farmers downstream becomes moot because there are no longer cost concerns to limit adequate water availability in any location regardless of natural river water flow.

For areas that are prone to the annual danger of wind damage due to hurricanes and tornados, it would make good sense for CEG manufacturers to consider using specialized designs that are more aerodynamically stable such as those used with aircraft fuselage and wing surfaces that tend to minimize air resistance.

In the case of CEGs in these areas, it would take a very rare tornado or hurricane to do any significant damage if most of the wind energy is deflected away from the interior as long as there is a means to balance air pressure inside with the moving air on the outside surfaces.

Another related idea seems like a logically sound one and states that most any greenhouse construction could be built to have part of the interior put underground.

Obviously this idea works best for lower latitudes as well as during times of the year when the sun peaks higher in the sky to allow more direct or diffuse sunlight to impinge upon the entire plant crop areas within the CEGs.

CEGs based partially underground have the advantage of holding a more constant temperature day and night, and can maintain an optimized humidity with less effort for all crops that need higher humid conditions.

These types would work especially well for growing such things as bananas, coffee beans, avocados and many tropical fruits where the native growing areas need to be selected and maintained within a narrow range of control for humidity, temperature and optimized soil conditions that are present only in certain locations.

To control atmospheric conditions within CEGS, the challenge is to try to maintain semi-optimized day and night temperatures, humidity, carbon dioxide, adequate water and air flow free of toxic pollution.

Even insect problems could theoretically be maintained better in a controlled environment greenhouse because the use of anti-insect products could likely be minimized due to the restricted areas requiring less dispersion of whatever is used to control the harmful pests.

CEG technology could use specialized units for growth and storage of seeds of every imaginable variety as long as growing conditions are set up properly.

They could offer the advantage of having storage and production under the same roof in underground rooms and compartments to categorize every type and variety deemed practical for any location.

For more advanced operations, another idea comes as a natural for contributing to the health of the farm families by using a recycling system of pumping greenhouse air into a home environment to help maximize the oxygen content for the home, and then recycling the home air back to the CEG environment to give a higher content of carbon dioxide that the plants need to thrive day and night.

For suitable rural areas, CEGs can consist of customized designs of much larger surface area and interior volume to enable large expanses for the growth of fruit trees, grain and hemp that normally use extensive farming methods.

Smaller units using CEG technology will logically be adapted for growing a variety of herbs in various rooms with different soils, temperature, humidity and atmospheric control to optimize growing conditions.

The obvious advantages of CEG production include better quality control of products, on point distribution, and the extent of availability that import reliance cannot compete with due to cost concerns.

In theory, CEG farming could completely replace the need for any extensive farm production once the technology evolves to its maximum potential.

Even so, there might still be some products that would do just as well with ordinary methods such as wheat, corn, hemp, cashews, bamboo, potatoes, etc. which implies that both methods have their advantages according to locality and preference to select which method or combination of both might be most feasible.

From one growing season to the next, crop rotation and supplemental nutrients can be utilized quite effectively in CEG farming the same way as accomplished in large acreage operations to keep the soil more optimized for consistency in quality and extent of production.

By using an extra abundance of CEGs in their locality, farmers can choose to let some growth rooms stay unused for a certain amount of time to allow a pattern of artificially induced 'growing seasons' to balance out supplies to prevent over or under abundance of any type of crop that a farmer wishes to specialize in.

CEGs can be designed for installation using a variety of customized modular panels in the walls and ceilings to allow only a certain ratio of direct sunlight to pass through for the effect it has on efficiency of plant growth

In some cases, this concept could work well to reduce excess direct sun during the warm summer days, and allow easily replaced panels of greater clarity for more sunlight to enter during the colder seasonal days of winter.

25 Controlled Environment Greenhouses

Similar to large food producers that now operate under the money-driven concept of extensive growth for profit by canning or freezing, CEG farmers could also use canning or freezing methods for local distribution without a constraint of profit to complicate an otherwise efficient operation.

Using CEGs, any homeowner having sufficient acreage and climate conditions could theoretically install several (or even many) separate units on the property surrounding the home in a convenient pattern that would allow the hiring of farm hands to work all year around.

The advantages of creating employment for local food manufacturing businesses having a small canning or freezing facility on the premises is obvious.

The added efficiency of such operations for 'on the spot sale' to the local residents within a limited distance to minimize cost of distribution would be enormous.

The ideas just expressed in this chapter were thought of a very long time ago but were effectively suppressed by the profit-driven motivation of the wealthy few at the expense of preventing long term advantages for everyone else.

With a ShareFlow ECU network that would replace the capitalistic way of doing things in America and other nations stalled by accepting the ultra-conservative world view of life, an inconvenient truth will surely emerge that the human race can no longer tolerate a business as usual attitude.

~26~
ECU Qualifications

Since earned credit units would be dispensed only to those holding a status of employment deemed to be useful to society in general, an obvious question is: How are the number of credit units for a specific type of employment and extent of assignments determined?

Certainly credit units will need to be dispensed equitably and fairly for everyone and will necessarily vary from person to person according to their job description.

From a broad overview of the compensation process, it seems apparent that whatever method is used to determine proper salary for any worker must be done in a manner that eliminates the iconic realities of the money-driven world.

Just as the SANE monetary approach would put a lid on the maximum income any one individual or corporation could acquire in terms of net worth, so also would the ECU network of credit units need to put an irrevocable cap on the maximum number of credit units that any profession or type of work could qualify for.

And since the low end of ECU quantification is already accounted for in terms of automatic coverage of the basics of subsistence (food, clothing, shelter, health care, etc.), once upper limits are determined, there should be a linear ratio of earned credit unit allocations for every work status between the extremes of upper and lower income.

For example, the average middle class worker in today's world doing the same type of work they are accustomed to would be assigned an appropriate number of credit units to allow a basically 'middle class' affordability for purchasing within a wide range of comfortable living affluence in terms

214

of goods and services, but not to exceed or drop below what is reasonable according to the value of their employment.

In any case, the high-priced income designees of today's world such as sports stars, actors, attorneys, real estate and investment brokers, managers, CEO's, politicians, etc. could be disallowed any additional credit units determined to be inconsistent with one's true contributory value.

Similarly at the low end of today's money-driven world of stressful labor without proper compensation, the number of ECU credit units issued to them could be adjusted to give them the boost they deserve in terms of the true value they have earned as a result of their contribution to the welfare of society in general.

The requirement that all credit units dispensed as wages must be based upon calculations that determine the actual number of units to be issued for each job description,   and should default to zero when necessary to disqualify types of work that seem to have no recognizable benefit to anyone.

Specifically the quantification of credit units would need to sensibly disallow any dispensations for wages applied to job descriptions determined to be of neutral value or actually detrimental to the common good.

Any attempt to legalize employment value based upon religious ideology cannot of itself be used to justify certain employment situations that prove harmful or detrimental to the rights of others.

Sensible restraints need to be in place to protect the right of every citizen to pursue their inalienable rights of life, liberty and the pursuit of happiness as long as those rights do not adversely affect the rights of others.

There are some job descriptions that are accepted in today's cultures that prove to be detrimental or disrespectful to some even as interpretations may vary from one culture to the traditional perceptions of others.

In any case, it is easy to list a few that are questionable in all cultures in spite of popular acceptance by many based upon well-grounded traditions that can put them in denial of the harm their occupations could cause for others.

These businesses include those that produce hard liquor, tobacco, dangerous weapons touted as necessary for self-defense, drugs and substance abuse distributors including businesses that can legally produce and distribute marijuana for purposes that infringe on the rights of others.

The list could go on to include casinos and operations involved in other forms of addictive gambling because even though each of these are legal and respond to customers by choice, the result tends to promote activities that are often detrimental to partners in a relationship as well as children in families often creating emotional and mental illness that can spill over to create other problems.

In other words, occupations such as the ones listed can produce fallout that can at the very least be called disrespect for the rights of others and can create harm to many who are closest to the ones employed in these operations.

These and other employment descriptions involving the production and distribution of products and services that disrespect the rights of others should logically be disqualified for ECU credit compensations on the basis of the definition of useful employment.

By default, workers involved with these job types should be qualified only for the free subsistence basics of life just like individuals who are unemployed or disabled.

Such a philosophy as the foundation of a moneyfree world is logical and based upon a necessity to exclude any job descriptions that would end up falsely construed as value earned for value given to benefit the common good.

The philosophy of exclusion in the ECU network of earned credit units means that anything determined to be self-harming, harm to others or disrespect of the rights of others to obtain unauthorized credits would be disallowed.

With respect to transactions that involve purchase of products and services, it would make sense to disallow ECU credits to be used for anything generally accepted as being harmful such as liquor, tobacco, illegal drugs and other addictive substances, abusive use of prescription drugs or excessive use of over-the-counter medications or any other products proven to be harmful to self or others.

Likewise, by the very nature of substances proven to be harmful to society, the logical conclusion of issuance of credit units by reason of value given only for value earned should disallow the support of any products or services that inflict harm to society, and thereby encourage all workers in these occupations to seek alternate employment.

With the ShareFlow ECU network in operation for an economy set up to respond for the common good of all, employment in fossil fuel development could not exist.

Any companies producing illegal drugs or even tobacco products would not be subsidized or supported in any way since no money would exist, and the rules of the ShareFlow network would disallow it.

Compensation for illegal or unethical services such as suppression of renewable clean energy products, political influence, spying, or meddling in the affairs of local, state or national interests to unethically benefit an individual or a group of individuals would not be allowed.

Over the entire spectrum of global occupations, the ECU network would pay wages only to workers in qualified beneficial employment and accept payments only for goods and services qualified to benefit the common good.

And the bottom line for eligibility when issuing ECU credits would be assurance that only ethical transactions are part of the system and that the issuance of credit units must be secured to record the identities of everyone involved in any transaction in order to automatically reject any transfer attempted in a fraudulent manner.

What may come to mind at this point is how existing money accounts that hold invested dividends, inheritance wealth and other sources of income from family inheritance, equities, trusts, loan payments from other individuals, etc. are to be interpreted when converting to earned credit units.

This would appear to allow conversion of perhaps large sums of money in accounts where the money was not really earned but needing to be converted to credit units of equal value that are qualified to be issued only to those whose gainful employment results in real benefits to society.

Holding to the philosophy of value received for value earned, there would need to be rules to determine values of existing money accounts that could be analyzed to separate qualified fractions of totals identified as previously earned money or at least amounts that were justifiably acquired by the account holders in exchange for equivalent credit units.

By following that rule, the remaining residual of funds in every money account should be disqualified for conversion and would be discarded in order to adhere to the philosophy of using credit units as the exclusive medium of exchange.

For example, let us take the case of a wealthy husband and wife now retired and living on retirement income that consists of a total of 10 million dollars in their two separate accounts at the same bank.

To keep this example simple, let us say that 5.5 million of that sum was inherited from the wife's deceased family and that 4.5 million consisted of savings and investments that the husband and wife accrued together as a result of 25 years of employment at the Space Systems Alliance Corporation.

Accordingly, the ECU network rules that the 4.5 million dollars is eligible for conversion to ECU credits, but the 5.5 million remaining in their accounts should disappear since it was handed down through inheritance and not considered as earned by the recipients.

Result: The 4.5 million dollars is converted to credit units and placed as equal shares into the personal accounts of both husband and wife who now have their total net worth residing in the ShareFlow ECU banking system.

Let's consider some other reasons that credit units need to be pre-qualified before being automatically released to the appropriate accounts of the gainfully employed.

Since an ECU debit card would be used for purchase of all goods and services, what happens when a card is lost or stolen is obviously a good question to consider.

We all know what happens when money is involved with ordinary credit and debit cards, but since the ShareFlow ECU system would work only with earned credit units, the network would have procedures to disallow fraudulent use.

If a card is lost or stolen, that card would be pre-coded and made permanently inactive once reported, and would be replaced with a new pre-coded card with the same access to the rightful owner, however the primary advantage to the account holder would be an automatic release from any accountability of payment over unauthorized usage.

If another person used the lost or stolen card before it became inactive, the rightful owner would be automatically compensated with the appropriate number of earned credit units placed back into their rightful account as soon as their lost or stolen card was reported.

With ShareFlow working only with earned credit units, there would be an automatic compensation to the rightful owner without ShareFlow having any concern over their payout since their 'loss' would not exist as accountable money in their infinite ocean of **yuna**.

The ShareFlow system could have other safeguards in place to ultimately identify a wrongful user and have that person tracked down and debited the amount of units used prior to the inactivation.

Any unlawful acquisition by a wrongful card holder would not result in a loss to the rightful card owner, because the purchases would not involve money, but simply earned credit units temporarily lost, but easily and quickly adjusted for rightful ownership when the loss was reported.

Consider an attempt to establish a non-existent business with fake employees that would get unauthorized credit units from the ECU network if not identified as such.

This situation would be effectively prevented by having periodic inspections of all businesses reported to ShareFlow so that any unlawful business status could be identified and shut down in a relatively short period of time.

The ShareFlow global banking system of earned credit units would be a sophisticated, yet completely transparent operation relative to the public at large so that fraudulent operations of any nature could be automatically flagged and prevented before any significant detrimental effect would occur to the rightful owners of accounts.

If a new business is developed that begins or appears to start out as a viable business venture and later develops into something that is proven to be unethical or harmful to the general population, there could be safeguards similar to a better business bureau filtering system that could be self-contained within ShareFlow as part of the banking system that would handle any complaints that might come in.

As soon as a significant number of complaints come in about any kind of business, there could be an inspection by employees of ShareFlow to determine if the complaints are justified enough to take action.

If they are, that business could be disqualified as such, and all employees operating under that business name might need to reapply for new accounts to begin with appropriate numbers of earned credit units that they rightfully have earned prior to their association with the discontinued and defunct business name.

If a legitimate business, corporation or division of local, state or national government is discovered to have non-existent employees as revealed through periodic inspections by ShareFlow, then the personal accounts of these identities would be immediately and permanently deactivated.

In this case, the owners or managers responsible for the fraudulent employee records would be appropriately fined by way of deletion of existing credit units in their personal accounts including a reduction of monthly allotments to make it untenable to garner fraudulently in this manner.

When a person becomes deceased, their personal earned credit unit accounts are deactivated so that all existing credit units in these accounts cease to exist and cannot be passed on to family or heirs because doing so would go against the principle of value given for value earned.

All these and many other similar examples illustrate the need for fairness and equality that must be maintained in a completely transparent manner to the public at large for the system to work successfully.

This would especially hold true for everyone at the forefront of acceptance of the earned credit system and to all those that become motivated to get it launched as a 'small step for man and a giant step for mankind'.

~27~
Responding to Problems

With respect to an ECU Network transition to replace our money-driven economy, any well-thought out design should include quick response and preventative maintenance actions to thwart problems of any nature that may threaten the integrity of the system.

Obviously this whole effort needs to be thought out well in advance by respected individuals in the financial world including individuals of high integrity to formulate a system on a small scale initially to provide time for testing response to all potential problems to confirm reliability and security.

An important part of the goal would be to have security measures in place for public scrutiny so that implementation can proceed on schedule with all system procedures well tested before the prototype network can become the new standard throughout the global economy.

There would probably be at least three significant areas where potential problems could arise even after the system is optimized and declared reliable.

One would be related to the effect of climate change and weather disasters possibly causing serious disruption or destruction of computerized records in any given locality that could hamper uninterrupted ECU transactions.

Another source of trouble is the obvious relationship of the system to the integrity of the management players who might have a disposition to use fraudulent means of gaining undue advantage for themselves at the expense of others.

Fortunately there could be adequate means to disallow fraud or environmental disruption from seriously interfering with the smooth operations by designing the fundamental nature of the network prior to implementation.

With respect to the first problem, by allowing all ECU documentation to be set up for redundant record storage in all other global network office locations, the loss of records in any one locale could be replaced by referring to any of the redundant locations operating throughout the system.

The worn out excuse of 'but that would cost too much!' is disposed of in its tracks because cost would no longer be a factor in any of the ECU network operations.

And since cost considerations would no longer be an issue in the ShareFlow ECU network, there could be a high priority for occupational assignment duties dealing with general problem response that would be part of the global network management team - trained and ready to respond at the time of the network launch.

As in any project involving security work assignments, proper resources of workers would need to be planned for, hired and given ECU earned credit status by reason of their employment to operate as maintenance personnel much like security jobs for operations at corporate and governmental facilities being needed for nonstop operations.

If network personnel at any level of work hierarchy have primary assignments that are not directly related to problem solving, their status could include on-call status to step in as necessary if a system problem arises that would need an immediate response for maintaining nonstop operations.

As an example, let us consider a typical tornado disaster that can occur unexpectedly in any town or city across the U.S. mainland that could destroy a local ECU network bank facility to where earned credit unit banking and verification of payments for product and service transactions would be temporarily disrupted.

And just like power out situations that electric power company personnel normally respond to, an ECU network service restoration in a serious storm disaster might require all available workers capable of helping to restore service to be on-call to aid their normal response teams regardless of what their regular employment assignments might be.

In situations like these, they could be trained to quickly provide bypass internet links to the redundant global system to maintain transaction operations until the infrastructure of normal local facilities are restored.

To address the possibility of an attempted fraudulent transaction, every operation involving an ECU earned credit account either in the issuing wage payment process or in the payback process for products and services would need to be handled in a secure hack-proof manner.

This process would need to be periodically checked for accuracy at all pertinent levels of responsibility by those with proper authority to guarantee hack-proof security for every transaction at all times.

It would also need to be completely transparent to the public at large to maintain their trust, support and assurance that the network is living up to all expectations throughout the global economic environment.

As always, this issue must be addressed in the planning stage prior to network implementation to eliminate serious surprises or compromise to respond to after the fact.

The personnel with this level of duty and occupational status would earn their respective ECU credits on the basis of a full time specialty in their job description focused solely on a 24/7 maintenance of network security at all pertinent levels to assure that no compromise occurs.

These workers would be assigned at every ShareFlow ECU bank locality redundantly connected to all other local banks in the network, and have the capability of staying in communication with others having the same responsibilities.

It would be a sub-network within the ECU network set up globally for the purpose of real-time system checks to assure that all links are working accurately and are free of outside interference, and that no problem can occur without the proper response.

But the greatest deterrent to fraud in the ShareFlow ECU network would be the process of effectively removing the incentives and motivation for involvement in resorting to fraudulent events prior to their occurrence.

This would occur by reason of the fact that ECU credits could only be acquired by those with qualified employment, which would then be disallowed for transfer to anyone else.

This stipulation alone would likely eliminate most of the incentive to try to commit fraud since no money is available for transfer, and no credit units could ever be transferred to an unqualified individual.

All ECU transactions, whether they would be for issuing credits to individuals or turning in credits for a purchased product or service could be recorded redundantly in the network worldwide so that any loss of information at any location could be restored through transfer from the nearest convenient network center.

The third source of potential trouble interfering with the smooth operation of credit unit transactions could occur at the point of activity in terms of breakdown of equipment and local system failure due to environmental compromise of the operational software or hardware.

In other words, equipment or software break down can happen unexpectedly no matter how perfect an installation begins their operation to start with.

This means that adequate backups of all software and hardware equipment would need to be available at the start of network launch for use if and when system interruptions requiring module replacement would occur.

For example, a common occurrence in today's money world is for a grocery or department store to temporarily shut down due to an unexpected event that can send the available software people scrambling to locate the problem and fix it as soon as possible.

27 Responding to Problems

When the store clerk is at the check stand to do a simple transaction of ECU credit units for a customer's purchase of goods such as food and other grocery items, the last thing the customer wants is a disruption to prevent the recording of the exchange and therefore impose an inconvenient wait time for the problem to be fixed.

One idea that might eliminate or at least minimize the number of such instances would be to have a redundant computer software pathway that can be used as a temporary override to complete the transactions in a semi-continuous manner while the problem with the original equipment is being studied, identified and fixed in the system electronics.

'Too costly for redundancy' would be the admonition of conservative business owners, but in an ECU network, a system design add-on like this would never be too costly since money would no longer be an issue

In any case, appropriate personnel would need to be on hand to respond at every location where ECU credit units are processed for purchase of goods or services.

For this purpose they would need to have their job duty descriptions either defined for this responsibility alone, or included with other employment responsibilities on a part time basis as needed.

On a full time responsibility basis, let's say there are X number of stores existing in a commercial mall setup that handle only ECU credit units in every transaction, and that two or three personnel have an office of their own to be on call at all times to respond to any or all stores in the mall in case of system interruption or breakdown.

This would make sense and be justified in the ECU economy as long as these personnel perform their on-call duties in a responsible and efficient manner similar to how firemen, police officers, and other response personnel need to perform their duties.

Just like any other types of employment, these positions would need adequate compensation and income in the form of **yuna** earned credit units based on their work history, skills and work load requirements.

Today's money-driven conservatives might stamp their foot and holler at all these ideas with their usual palaver that redundancy setups in the work force always cost too much.

Their arguments fall flat however when they finally learn that costs can no longer be used as a valid excuse when the system no longer uses money or profit as a consideration.

Simply planning for the proper amount of workers and work related effort to respond to problems considered in the ECU network development stage should unequivocally avoid the notion that redundancy costs too much as long as these redundancies are determined necessary to maintaining long-term efficiency and reliability.

~28~
A Cooperative World Government

Ultimately we will have a united one-world government that is based upon cooperation and trust among all nations, but first we must convince the people of all nations and their leaders that such an effort is possible and sustainable.

Consider SECO as an acronym to designate what I call a Self-Construct Co-Operacy government arising from the phase-out of all money-driven economic systems that are replaced by the ShareFlow ECU network economy free of the slavery of money accountability.

Self-Construct means it will support and maintain the initiatives created by the citizens that aspire to create self-improvement over time in a fully self-corrective manner.

The Co-Operacy part of this description stands for a fully global commitment of cooperation to work together to make good things happen for all the people and not just the top echelon of the wealthy elite.

The SECO Government I illustrate is only a suggested model for a world government structuring based upon a logical analysis that would combine the best features of capitalism along with the dynamics of a new foundation of government known as compassionate socialism working together as a logical alternative to existing structures.

The top priority of this description is to fully retain all inalienable human rights and freedoms as guaranteed by the U.S. Constitution and Bill of Rights, while providing consideration for necessary additions or modifications from time to time resulting from the evolution of a changing global society.

228

28 A Cooperative World Government

The intent is not to define an ideologically perfect or unachievable and unworkable fantasy, but to explore and invite new ideas for setting in motion a series of steps and makeover towards a sensible world government that is fair, trustworthy and equitable to all including every man, woman and child on the planet.

The intent is to have it designed in such a manner as to provide every citizen equal opportunities, equal rights and equal freedoms, with every person considered of equal value regardless of race, gender, ethnic background, age, religion or net worth in terms of wealth or status.

One of the ways this objective can be accomplished is to use concepts from existing realities with the intent to construct a matrix of small habitats to test and integrate socioeconomic concepts in closed systems.

Successful manifestation on a small scale with careful design, testing and documentation can then be expanded to larger systems and eventually a workable universal network built upon public education, trust and awareness that a cooperative government is really a good idea.

Not just a good idea, but with a powerful desire for global cooperation as the driving force, it would be the only logical solution to the problems of a world fraught with out-of-control chaos, frustration, misunderstandings and lack of trust that would eventually result in far greater advantage for the common good of all.

Using the results and success of various small system habitats as a springboard, the entire concept of a globally based SECO Government linked with related economic structuring known as the ShareFlow ECU network could then be tested for a gradually expanding scope basis.

These test modules could be set up to integrate with an expected increase in the number of developing habitats, along with an increase in scope of each cooperative system throughout the global environment.

229

28 A Cooperative World Government

The end game would likely be a feasible transition to a compassionate global government and economy working together that would replace all existing governments and socioeconomic systems with the means to have all benefit with even greater freedom and human rights over time.

The creation of a new and separate internet operating in parallel with the existing one possibly known as UniNet might work well for the purpose of communication to and from all SECO facilities and all ShareFlow branch offices throughout the system, wherein all the necessary links are made accessible to all citizens for assurance that the entire operation is working to their benefit.

UniNet would have to be carefully designed and set up as basically hack proof with redundant security measures, and be freely transparent and open to everyone to monitor how the new government is operating at all times.

In lieu of existing executive offices such as president, prime minister, governor, etc., I see each nation state as having their executive branch consisting of a governorship of three presiding officers.

Each of the three would hold equal and redundant authority to make decisions affecting their specific extent of population, and would be elected by that portion of citizens under their jurisdiction through UniNet voting.

A similar structuring for executive governments at province, district and locality levels would also be a logical set up for similar and efficient government operations.

In lieu of having a conventional legislative branch of government for each nation state, the law-making branch at each level of government would simply consist of a redundantly documented global database of all laws and advisories already created by input from the voting public.

All laws would be scrutinized for accountability to uphold the rights of every citizen, and thus be retained or discarded depending upon their value to the citizens.

Most laws would be considered mandatory, but some laws could be given a non-binding status called advisories, which then become discretionary suggestions and be open for common sense interpretation whenever necessary.

The legislatures would be set up to allow every world citizen to have continuous UniNet access to review every piece of documented legislation.

Every citizen would have the right to help decide directly what should or should not be part of the charter of existing laws and advisories relevant to each individual's area of jurisdiction.

A judicial branch of government would consist of a simplified structure using a global database of laws and advisories that would specify logical means of determining guilt or innocence, and would employ judges that could refer to that part of the database specifying accountability of citizens for their actions.

All of this structuring would depend upon a common sense philosophy to target true justice in every situation rather than being subject to perennial gridlock by legalese and money-influenced lawyers attempting to always win a case using technicalities, unethical strategies and loopholes in their awkward attempts to sidestep true justice.

The basis of the entire SECO government would be to form a habitat of responsibility composed of ethically minded individuals that can govern with incentives to encourage everyone to cooperate fully for improvement as changes occur over time.

As new information is available to access for changing social, environmental and economic situations, necessary adjustments can be made by vote from the citizens using their secure input via the UniNet.

All information would be transparent to the public at large and could be used to decide who is best qualified for nomination for election to public offices at all levels.

UniNet technology would be used to decide which aspiring candidates are best qualified to hold office, and would count voting input from the citizens in respective jurisdictions to elect those they feel are best to fulfill the responsibilities at each of their global, national, state and local levels of responsibility.

All candidates for office at local, state, national and global levels of authority would be given equal funding for campaign expenses by ShareFlow, and in so doing would disallow any contributions from any other source.

All campaign funding and financial support for each candidate would necessarily be fully accountable to the citizens affected by each office holder.

For a global government to function properly, we would likely need a restructuring of national boundaries and jurisdictions into a more efficient and viable system.

I envision this new form of government to be an all-inclusive global entity and have jurisdiction over all nation states eliminating all existing capitalistic regimes, socialistic constructs and dictatorships claiming ownership of land purporting to be an exclusively nationalistic regime.

The idea behind the SECO concept is simple, logical, a natural and an essential part of the formula for evolving socioeconomic changes whose time has come to take over responsibilities for a compassionate world community.

There would need to be a pilot project that could test out the ramifications of the ShareFlow ECU network and the SECO government networking together on a minimal scale to start with, but one that could easily be expanded in response to adequate public education.

Once initial testing is complete, there would probably be a great demand for adding additional test locations so that the logistics of setting up the grand scheme globally would be wholly feasible and relatively easy to accomplish.

Not only would the systems of the SANE economy under ShareFlow and the SECO government dynamics be documented in their test phases, but also how the human element of differing sets of values, philosophies, cultures, ideologies and lifestyles in mutual cooperation would be successfully integrated and accounted for.

To learn to cooperate and function successfully in a temporarily closed society might be the initial goal of the restructuring so that principles necessary for a successful implementation on a global scale could be documented, evaluated and set up at the appropriate time.

One suggestion for the testing phase would be to set aside four years for participants to live together in several biosphere environments in order to test all aspects of the support systems necessary in a mini-SECO and ShareFlow network operating exclusively within the enclosures.

Another four years could then be used to resolve any problems and begin an expanded testing phase for a more extensive operational phase to coordinate activities for all biosphere participants into an interactive community.

During that time, all biosphere participants would be essentially cut off from the outside world to disallow any compromise of the closed prototype system testing.

Over eight years of testing SECO and SANE working together, there could be development of a comprehensive initiative to provide education aimed at the general global population to prepare for universal network operations.

If education is sufficient, it would be logical to assume support from millions of citizens all over the world who would want to become the next participants in one of the follow-up projects.

Done properly, this would allow for a slow growth and expansion of the original model communities, and provide for a gradual and secure expansion into a fully operational global network of ShareFlow and SECO government to operate with **yuna** earned credit units instead of money.

By doing so, all traditional governments would be put into an acceptable phase out allowing for a corresponding phase in of the new world model and gradual replacement of existing nations with SECO structures and operations.

Even though a compassionate global system would be very logical for implementation, the concept would still be resisted with the illogical fury of conservative thinking.

For awhile anyway…

Therefore it would make good sense to prepare and present effective educational presentations to the populace of all existing nations and cultures regarding the inevitable phase out of existing governments including communism, capitalism, socialism, monarchies and plutocracies.

Without a SECO and SANE cooperative to take over, conservative societies would continue to maintain their lack of trust and mind-set that the clash of cultures within a money-driven world could never learn to work together to bring about workable and sensible innovations because it would always 'cost too much' (being the standard cliché and excuse to maintain money slavery over the masses).

Does it not boggle the mind on how the lack of vision of a relatively few in power (a plutocracy and oligarchy over everyone else) continue to short-circuit the hopes and dreams of the masses to bring about the necessary changes that would benefit everyone including those who resist?

Is it not their shortsightedness and stifling mindset of their need for profit, control and fear tactics that always prevent any real change that the masses inherently know would benefit everyone?

I certainly think it is!

The accountability of money is paramount worldwide, but the accountability for spiritual values and responsible governing from our leaders is always hard to come by.

Another factor of existing economic and social malaise is simply dysfunctional government control because the system that was originally set up has deteriorated based upon the culture of division and distrust of our neighbors.

It comes into play when any government gets heavy-handed and arrogantly imposes their knee-jerk imposition of creating unnecessary laws or preventing sensible reform due to their gridlock that ignores intelligent discussion.

Quite often governments provide only band-aid and self-interest solutions to economic and social problems to appease the masses temporarily.

For endless generations, frenzied competition has allowed a relatively few to acquire most of the wealth to misuse economics and create moneyclot to prevent the efficient flow of money through the economy.

And just like a massive blood clot in a living organism, moneyclot of one form or another has often degraded and killed off many worthwhile projects that unrestricted flow of money through the economy is supposed to nourish.

Progressives understand that government should have only two basic and prioritized functions:

1. It should manage the policies of operation that the citizens decide should be established and upheld, and

2. It should only pass laws that uphold the rights and freedoms guaranteed to everyone but do not adversely affect the rights and freedoms of anyone else.

Any attempt to impose control of economics, social mores or codes of morality is not the rightful business of any government at any level.

Rather, it is each government's duty to protect citizen's rights, incentives and motivation to pursue one's personal goals and choice of lifestyle free of unethical interference.

This includes the right to life, liberty and the pursuit of happiness without using religion or personal philosophy to infringe upon the rights or freedoms of anyone else.

The simplistic admonition of 'too much government' has been a deep-seated notion and fallacy that says no government leader should ever be trusted.

28 A Cooperative World Government

It is apparent that in general, the governments of all nations tend to create a lot of laws but resist beneficial policies that encourage free money flow to everyone.

This blocks efficient productivity and tends to wipe out incentives to produce high quality goods and services.

Many people soon begin to realize that working hard is no longer worth the effort.

Over time, government erodes into favoring influential politicians and wealthy corporate heads at the expense of most everyone else.

But we already know that, right?

In their mindless pursuit of self-interest, the privileged cultures camouflage the real problems of moneyclot, profit motive, destructive competition, power to manipulate and control others, and the imbalances resulting in inefficient development and distribution of products and services.

Economic problems seem so monumentally complex right now that any spontaneously proposed solution seems to serve only as an ineffective band-aid treatment at best.

It is now time for all of us to see the whole picture and get proper perspectives of the higher and greater truths.

Some progressives now understand that we can retain many of the proven sensible aspects of capitalism, and still incorporate other ideas proven practical in compassionate socialistic movements within governments.

To prove that SECO and SANE could integrate and work together successively, it would seem logical to test all functions illustrating a model of cooperative government and efficient economics as proposed so it could operate as a mini-prototype for documentation and presentation to interested citizens of all nations and cultures.

This initiative could be the foundation of what could eventually become the accepted form of a united world government consisting of carefully defined nation states with logically defined land divisions for more efficient structuring.

28 A Cooperative World Government

In my subsequent description of the structuring of a hypothetical world government, I have suggested creating an arbitrarily chosen set of 256 nation states, quite simply known as The United States (or Nations) of Earth.

The acronym of U.S.E. or U.N.E. would then replace and encompass all existing national boundaries and be set up with a comprehensive global Constitution as a basis for progressive changes in a self-correcting manner.

SECO and SANE working together in a unified global system using the ShareFlow ECU network of earned credit units instead of traditional money would then define a new world paradigm to use only clean energy resources such as solar, wind, hydrogen storage and zero point energies for sustaining a pristine environment and forever banish the dependency of fossil fuel usage.

This new vision of future government and economics could begin a sustainable movement towards improving living standards, greater personal freedom, and reduced quantity, yet more quality and efficiency in government and economics for the citizens of all nation states.

It would establish a basis for continuous improvement in quality of life for the masses and would be set up to stay in harmony with the forces of nature and prepare for the challenges of a changing global civilization.

~29~
One World Language

With a global community eventually united under a one-world government, the logic of having a universal language common to everyone would seem beyond 'a natural', and in fact shouts loud and clear as a priority for allowing SECO and SANE to operate with optimum efficiency.

As opposed to what may have happened ages ago at the tower of Babel leading to the proliferation of a plethora of language variations and challenges to clear communications, it makes sense to say we are ready for something different.

What if a new approach for efficient communication was considered that starts out with identifying all the factors that work together for overall efficiency in speaking, reading, writing and computer usage?

The next step might be an analysis of priorities that are identified to evaluate all efficiency factors to consider so that language models could be created out of existing languages for comparison and put out for public display and input regarding which model best suits the prioritized features.

With this in mind, it would make good sense to set up an international commission to design and create a universal language with all the desirable characteristics built in from the start, since the cost of developing a new language would no longer be a limiting factor with SANE economics.

Universal language ideas are not new of course, but what is new is the increased impetus that says now is the time to seriously consider creating an efficient language that most anyone could embrace and learn quickly to be worthy of being called universal in everyday communications.

29 One World Language

Operating equally well for all nations and localities, a new language should be applicable to computer operations and a useful consideration for overall efficiency in everyday business communications.

In a manner quite different from the way the English language has by default become the language in common use for the international community, I am proposing an alternate but well-planned language everyone could use that might help eliminate confusion between races, cultures, religions and diverging philosophies.

Having a universal language that everyone could learn easily could increase the motivation for cooperative ventures between nations so that a realistic goal of international peace could be attainable in a relatively short time.

This is not to say that a new language should eliminate the use of native languages now held in great esteem, but rather it should exist to be used as the common tool for all practical needs of communication adjusted to technologies in an evolving global community.

Referring to it simply as the **UL**, it could be designed for use as a side-by-side primary language along with an existing native tongue as the second means of communication for special needs as desired.

Apparently there was never a single source of authority to define all the rules of construction and grammar for any existing language when each was developed over time for practical everyday use.

Instead, various word structures and rules of grammar developed by the morphing of popular usage as defined by convenience occurred sporadically and unpredictably over the course of history to result in a plethora of ways to communicate that worked well for those adhering to the use of their own language of choice.

In doing so, each language fell short of an efficient way of bringing everyone together for the purpose of eliminating confusion between various races, nations and cultures.

29 One World Language

As a result, all existing languages fall short, and in many cases dramatically so from what could be considered easy flowing and optimal to express oneself clearly.

Natives and cultures developing their language through common use were forced to accept the limitation of built-in imperfections that could have been prevented if there had been a concerted effort to create a universal language with better efficiency by way of careful design.

Without a well-planned language in common use for everyone, the imperfections inevitably allowed the creation of unnecessary duplications, many awkward word structures redundancy, inaccuracies and misunderstandings that limit precise communication between users.

So what would the characteristics of an optimized way of communicating be and how would they be defined in a way as to create a language that is not only acceptable for the majority, but a lot of fun to learn and be constructed with rules to allow adaptability to new technologies and lifestyles?

How could a universal language be designed to adapt naturally to social, economic and technological changes that easily adjusts to new information and concepts that come along in the changing world of human experience?

Since the five aspects of communication are reading, writing, speaking, listening, and computer instruction code, a well-designed language should try to optimize all of these requirements in a balanced and concise manner.

The designers should consider maximizing efficiency while preserving qualities of literary ambiance that most citizens would logically prefer and call worthy of being seen as 'beautiful' and readily acceptable for their motivation to learn and use consistently.

Although no existing language has it all, the important variables of ambience, beauty, charm and efficiency can be recognized by studying other languages and applying useful principles in the design of the **UL** for all five aspects.

29 One World Language

The qualities of efficiency would include conciseness, ease of learning and a clear capability of adjusting to new concepts that our evolving global society would always need to define clearly.

Let us consider each of the five aspects separately, and take a brief look at what qualities should exist to make the language easy to adjust to and be gifted with the ambiance and beauty that all nations and cultures could appreciate.

For reading, the concepts of conciseness, free flowing and freedom from ambiguity seem to stand out as notable priorities for consideration.

In fact the process of creation could begin with the definition of a whole new alphabet with sensible rules to form concise words, phrases and complete thoughts.

The key change that I see for the **UL** would be to define every word and concept in units using an alphabet of single characters representing the complete sound of a **syl-la-ble** rather than being defined as separate vowels or consonants.

Since there are many syllables in common use made up of consonant and vowel combinations including all that begin with a consonant and end with a vowel and vice-versa, I suggest that the new alphabet should consist of 400 unique letters with each letter representing a complete syllable sound.

The use of this rule alone would allow most common words in everyday use to be made up of no more than four UL syllables, (hence four letters of the alphabet) without any unnecessary characters involved in word definitions.

In fact many of the most often used words we now have defined in English could then be defined in **UL** with only one letter representing a unique **syllable** sound.

Another suggestion would be to consider using specific letters in the new alphabet to begin different parts of speech by using a unique UL letters to differentiate between them.

For example, using a unique letter to begin all nouns, and another to begin all verbs, etc. and allowing a different letter in the new alphabet to begin all other parts of speech uniquely would seem to be an efficient structural advantage.

This would imply a unique letter to begin all pronouns, another for all adverbs, another for adjectives and another for prepositions, etc. so that the aspects of normal grammar would be identified on sight.

Another suggestion would be to use unique letters in the new alphabet to end words that need to show past or future tense definition, with the absence of both letters indicating the present tense.

That rule would conveniently define all verb usage on sight with the appearance of one of the letters at the end of the verb to define future tense usage, or the other letter at the end of the verb to define past tense usage.

These among other suggestions could make learning the language easier for greater memory retention by combining rules of grammar and definitions of words more efficiently.

Many have suggested that script writing has become less useful or even outdated due to computer and electronic means of communicating the printed word.

But what if the definition of the alphabet of syllables was purposely set up as being represented by combinations of strokes that resemble long-hand script writing that could easily interconnect with one another on a line of manually written or computerized text?

I envision a well-designed **UL** to consist of the use of any of the 400 syllable alphabet letters that uniquely define words and concepts in a long hand 'script' style to give it the quality of being called 'beautiful' with respect to the aspects of reading, writing and even computer usage.

The quality of 'beauty' in any language is noteworthy in romance languages such as Spanish and French because of the way the syllables of words seem to flow together when spoken or listened to.

For this reason, a flow of syllables instead of arbitrary consonant and vowel constructs could be used exclusively in designing each UL syllable letter so that no two consecutive consonant or vowel sounds are backed up together.

An example of that is to avoid constructing words like 'cop-stop' or 'cupcake'. A more flowing description might sound more like 'kah-stah' or 'kuh-pay' with syllable sounds flowing together as two-letter **UL** words.

The bottom line of a well-designed universal language is to illustrate the likelihood that a moneyfree economy could lend itself quite well to new innovations that are not possible in our existing money-driven profit motive reality.

As such, a universal language recognized and accepted by all nations in the global environment is not only a logical, efficient and easily learned transition for reading, writing, speaking and computer coding, but would likely become a priority goal for a cooperative one-world government.

The following are my suggestions for setting up the **UL** design rules once the ECU network is in operation and money limitations are no longer an issue.

/   Define the UL alphabet by creating the equivalent of 400 syllable letters using all the practical spoken sounds of syllables that are made up with only one single consonant and one single vowel sound for each letter.

/   Minimize the number of syllable letters in unique concepts for concise everyday conversation.

/   Use unique but simple script-like strokes to define each of the syllable-letters in the alphabet to make writing by hand more efficient when necessary.

/   Define words as unique concepts with no ambiguity of duplicate definitions for any word to minimize common misunderstandings in everyday conversation.

/   Define unique ideas by using only one word as the designation to reduce duplications and increase efficiency.

/   Define each letter to be connectable when writing words by hand or when letters are printed by computer so that speed reading is easily enhanced for the average reader.

29 One World Language

/ A simple space between words would suffice to enable easy recognition of unique concepts as words.

/ A special symbol to illustrate separation of sentences as unique expressions of thought for a rapid and easy way to enhance speed reading would also make good sense and adaptability to learn the language.

/ An alphabet of 400 unique letters as symbols lends to the logic that no word needs to be more than 4 letters in length, with most words needing only 1 or 2 letters.

/ Reserve the use of 3 or 4 letter words to describe medical, pharmaceutical and scientific terminology uniquely.

As technology expands to include new innovations and procedures for use in science and medicine, the need for greater conciseness becomes a priority for adaptation in all forms of communication.

Consider internet communication as one example.

Instead of having to use long word combinations for the designations of internet links as we often do now, the use of a universal language with an alphabet of 400 **UL** letters instead of 26 in the English language opens up a new world of concise possibilities that can increase efficiency in terms of time and word memory storage to allow link descriptions to be written more easily and coherently.

Instead of using **.com** or **.org** as domain descriptors for example, the use of just one letter in a 400 letter alphabet for all internet domains could suffice very nicely.

Likewise, with respect to the actual words that make up long link descriptions, the number of **UL** letters to retain uniqueness of a UR link could reduce to a small fraction of the number of letters usually required.

Many might balk at the idea of learning a whole new language and having to memorize 400 letters as opposed to using fewer letters in their native alphabet, however once **UL** is taught and used properly, the familiarity of everyday usage and ease of learning new communication skills should negate all serious objections.

29 One World Language

The idea of a universal language being a no-brainer with respect to sheer necessity in a world of advanced technology becomes a much greater possibility when the money-driven gridlock that suppresses new and sustainable ideas can no longer survive in an ECU network environment.

Indeed, it is our destiny that the gridlock will be cast aside in favor of floodgates of new innovations that can burst forth at every level of the socioeconomic structure.

And as such, it is a destiny that will dramatically allow a plethora of alternatives to take hold and prosper in a strange new world called mutual cooperation and moneyfree trust among all hands on deck who are more than willing to roll up their sleeves to get necessary projects completed that will benefit all of humanity and not just the wealthy elite.

~30~
256 Nation States

As the world population evolves to become more united and technologically advanced in a global economy, would it be illogical to think that all nations could eventually unite in some way for the purpose of creating a world government that is neither fearsome nor oppressive?

And would it be illogical to assume that a benevolent authority could be installed and motivated to keep it that way even if an effort in that direction would be promptly declared out of the question by conservative thinking?

It seems that any world government structure over all nations will continue to be condemned as unthinkable as long as the conflict of ignorance and fixations over religion, race and culture go unopposed and unchallenged.

Why is it that we have about 200 separate countries in the world that have developed rather haphazardly, and may have had their existence based upon a history of conflict over customs, religion, money, resources and land that the leaders of nations have imposed upon their citizens?

What if the purpose of separate nations was for setting up logical divisions that were not contentious for culture, race or economic conflict, but simply designed to make life mutually beneficial for every citizen to communicate, travel, do business and have social interaction more efficiently to maximize the quality of life for everyone?

What if nations could be designed with proper laws to help eliminate poverty, unnecessary occupations, crime, ill health, etc. while improving the quality of life for everyone and preventing wealthy controllers from imposing their will upon the masses at the expense of the less fortunate?

And wouldn't this conversation suggest that a concept whose time has come is here with a vengeance?

Although binding treaties define the legality of national borders, they do relatively little to define the real values that could ensue if every nation on Earth were to commit to total cooperation with their neighbors for the long term benefits of peace, economic abundance, quality of life, abolition of war, and sharing of control with responsible world leaders.

A dream by some (considered the impossible dream by many) is to unite all nations under one government that is not only compassionate for all citizens of all nations, but one that would be governed in such a way as to be sustainable and self-improving for future generations.

It would be sustainable by way of social and economic responsibility that all functions of the system would operate under what could be called a self-construct methodology.

Since most nations in today's global environment consist of partitioned states that are supposed to allow localities to operate more efficiently, a natural extension of the idea for a world government would be to have well designed partitions beginning with nation states to replace what we now think of as separate countries in today's fractured world.

It would mean dismantling the self-destruct dynamics of the system we have today with a long term goal of gradual replacement of money dependency with a moneyfree way of doing business that can operate responsibly without the need for strict money accountability.

That is why I am suggesting that world leaders will need to think about valuing the mutual benefits of a new world government that sets up a logical and well-organized way of structuring to enable all races, cultures and religions to live side by side in a basically peaceful fashion.

I see it as a benevolent system that would be capable of attending to the primary problems of economic inequality and injustice that is clearly tied to the increasing gap between the haves and the have-nots.

It is quite clear that the have-nots have no practical or effective way to create meaningful changes on their own since they do not have the resources and organization that money affords to the wealthy for creating changes that could benefit all including the top 1%.

Beneficial change that could allow logical distributions of wealth and resources cannot be established as long as the system allows money and the authority to control policies to suppress any dramatic change from ever happening.

This in turn allows the wealthy to operate with no desire to moderate their status quo, enabling them to dictate what everyone else must do under their profit-motive competitive way of doing business.

With the advent of a major two-step approach to create the ShareFlow ECU network of yuna earned credit units that gets money as we know it out of the dynamics, I suggest a hypothetical phase into a social structure that consists of 256 nation states with a one-world government referred to simply as United Nation States of Earth or the UNSE.

With a global cooperative effort among existing world leaders in any foreseeable future, The UNSE would need to be carefully planned and end up with a logical partitioning of existing nations and land masses into a more common sense division of boundaries.

It should be done in such a way as to promote equality between all existing nations so that all resources of necessity and management operations can become freely distributed and shared efficiently between all nation states.

The goal would be to establish the UNSE as sustainable for every citizen of any race, religion, culture or philosophy in a benign cooperative of global operations having all the social and economic rights and privileges that a government of the people, by the people and for the people is supposed to be based upon and maintain.

With our existing money-based system of inefficiency and mistrust of our neighbors, such a system is not possible.

With an ECU network system of earned credit units to replace all forms of money that we now depend upon, many things become possible, sensible, logical and much easier to consider when the motivation is to think outside the box and cooperate for the benefit of all.

A logical conclusion but when studied more carefully, the logic and good sense of suggesting it now as being the wave of the future becomes undeniable as it begins to slip through the entrenched thinking of many who feel it is only an unworkable pipe dream of the naive.

With money and money accountability taken out of the equation, a baseline of discussion for revolutionary changes becomes more likely when benefits of the end game can be demonstrated to the masses and their leaders.

With that in mind, I submit some ideas for uniting the world into 256 logically planned nation states to replace the chaotic structuring of approximately 200 nations now operating under an eternal struggle over money, land and control that would make much better sense as a global entity of common bond and trust.

The declaration that good things are likely to happen will fall into place naturally when the citizens and leaders of existing nations are given enough wakeup calls with a follow up of appropriate education.

Classes for all age levels can be set up to demonstrate the benefits that can occur when a free flow of resource sharing and international cooperation is allowed to manifest.

The choice of 256 replacement nation states is simply a suggestion, since the actual number could be different; but considering the total land area on Earth and the way nations are laid out now, that number seems like a good choice.

The idea of 256 countries operating under a one-world government structure would allow for a more realistic and workable creation of nation states under one cooperative

249

with a new comprehensive Constitution that would reflect more precise justice and be applicable to all their citizens.

It would take in the totality of all the habitable land areas now in existence by re-partitioning to make up the proposed nation states in order to have more sensible structuring in cases where there is non-contiguous land or ill-conceived boundaries that can create problems.

This suggestion is what I envision a logical structuring might look like and be set up to allow the world capitol to exist redundantly in each nation state capitol so that each of the 256 nation states could experience similar benefits and responsibilities of being designated to operate as the Capitol of the United Nation States of Earth.

Allowing this redundancy could be a powerful force to unite all nation states as one in spirit and purpose, and be an incentive to encourage and maintain global cooperation between all lifestyles and cultures.

Doing so could encourage free exchange of immigration from every nation to allow any citizen to relocate for more optimum settlement according to their cultural preference.

Without a system of money to confuse and corrupt all levels of government, the idea of a world authority is taken out of the 'impossible dream' classification and placed squarely on the table of priority, especially after those in authority are effectively educated as to why the phase-over is needed for the good of the planet.

Regarding a proposed structuring within each of the 256 nation states, the following suggestions describe a simple and straightforward manner of how a sensible partitioning of subdivisions could be defined.

A creation of a union of world nation states to replace all existing nations and land areas throughout the world could assign island territories in a logical manner as to be either included within the nearest nation state or become a new nation state in its own right.

Obvious examples include such island groupings we presently identify as the Hawaiian Islands, the Philippines, Polynesia, Micronesia, and Melanesia, etc.

By reassigning island groups like these as new nation states for proper recognition and representation, they are put on an equal status for sharing the social and economic resources available to any nation state, and could become an active part of the alliance that all nation states would need to commit to full cooperation for the common good.

For a typical number of divisions within each state, there might be divisions consisting of 16 provinces similar to the states that operate within existing nations.

For the next level down we could have assignments of districts similar to counties having equivalent functions as necessary divisions for localized government levels.

Further breakdown could include existing and future localities we presently define as cities, towns and villages to complete the makeup of land assignments while all ocean territories would still be unassigned up to a sensible distance from the shores of any newly defined nation state.

Since all maritime areas as well as territories of nation states would grant free access to all residents of any nation state, the contention over fishing rights or any other reason to question the right of free access to the open seas would no longer exist in a SECO government organization.

As an example of nation state land assignments, we can visualize what North America might look like if the existing countries of Canada, the United States and Mexico were reapportioned into a number of fairly equally divided land areas of 20 nation states.

The hypothetical breakdown could apportion the entire land area for reassignment as new nation states with logically defined boundaries using rivers or other naturally occurring land barriers for definitions as borders in each case.

The existing provinces of Canada, the large island mass of Greenland and the state of Alaska might be redefined as separate nation states including islands that exist but are not well defined above the Arctic Circle.

Another example would have Mexico divided into two or three nation states while Central America could have their separate countries redefined as nation states to make up the totality of North America's redistricting.

Examples of state reassignments in the U.S.A. could include California, Oregon, Washington, Arizona, Nevada, Utah and Idaho made up together as a new nation state.

In similar fashion, another reassignment of contiguous land could tag Montana, Wyoming, Colorado, New Mexico, Oklahoma and Texas as one nation state.

All other contiguous land areas within the United States could follow a natural assignment in logical combinations to create new nation states for a final total of 20 in the North American continent under a one world government.

The actual breakdown would necessarily be constrained to consider many variables for a stabilized arrangement in the global environment in order to meet a pre-assigned goal of 256 nation states which would obviously be an arbitrary number but a logical and manageable one.

As you will see in my next chapter entitled: A Universal Metric System, I choose the number 256 as the logical total of countries that makes good sense when a universal metric system based upon hexadecimal Base 16 is proposed instead of our Base 10 number system.

I advocate Base 16 for a number of reasons explained in the next chapter that bases the proposed transition as part of a moneyfree revolution of unlimited possibilities.

Continuing our hypothetical breakdown of land areas, we might assign Hawaii and Cuba with its accompaniment of nearby islands as separate nation states in spite of their relatively small land areas.

This reasoning would be based upon their construct and isolation as they now exist, while the logic for small states such as Maine, Vermont, New Hampshire, Massachusetts,

Connecticut and Rhode Island might also be combined to exist as one of the new 256 world nation states.

Another suggestion for a nation state creation coming to mind would be the combination of two nations as one such as Israel and Palestine being united with obvious benefits to the cultures of both once their respective leaders see the true benefits of getting over their age-old hatred and contentions between one another.

In spite of this animosity, the logic of combining them speaks loud and clear since the total land area making up either one is insufficient to adequately support their people in terms of resources and easy access to free mobility using available waterways.

And since the creation of 256 nation states would likely depend upon an established ShareFlow ECU network as the basis for economic justification and serious consideration, many related concepts can become reality even as they were previously relegated to the depths of impossibile mythology.

For example, if a proposed nation state designation is pointed out as being underpopulated, it would make good sense to encourage immigration by giving incentives to all sides for helping to balance numbers and resources.

Immigration out of the more populated regions and into areas previously thought unfavorable for living conditions could be given the necessary resources to expand and extend agricultural pursuits and overall resource development.

However a reapportionment would turn out as a new construct of 256 nation states, the idea would be to partition all large countries into smaller ones that are geographically intact with the result that all existing nations end up as part of an optimum creation of 256 nation states.

The bottom line of this logic is intended to help create a global cooperative with a benign world government that is authorized and commissioned to maintain the peace and the cooperative union of all nations in preventing future wars by maintaining a level playing field so that every global citizen can pursue and attain a reasonably high standard of living.

A benevolent world government presiding over logically defined nation states could go a long way to ensure that all world citizens can experience not only realistic pursuits of their dreams, but have standards of living consistent with maintaining equal opportunities for everyone.

Even more importantly, that government could provide the means to maintain a global environment that survives economically and ecologically in order to ensure that all life forms have the means to live free of the spectre of calamities that threaten the existence of our entire global civilization.

Once a final configuration of nation states is defined and agreed upon to fix boundaries and borders, each state could set up an embassy complex to where each of the other nation states is given access for representation in order to provide for optimized communications and total cooperation at all levels of government.

Each embassy would be designed to work together with all others to help solve global problems and ensure that all functions of government are consistent with user friendly and cooperative response to the needs of every citizen.

The world capitol location could be located redundantly in every nation state embassy to enable each nation to take their turn at presiding globally and making decisions that consider important world and national interests.

Within each world capitol location there could reside separate individuals having the same authority as if only one of them held an exclusively elected office of President of the United States of Earth.

This could ensure such that no nation state would be left out in decisions that affect the entire global community.

The initial structuring logic would give official status to redundant world leaders who would periodically share the same responsibilities each would have if only one of them presided as the world leader.

Each of these officials would obviously need to be well-qualified for their redundant office and responsibilities of ensuring that all global citizens have the freedoms, human rights, respect and equal treatment they deserve regardless of race, religion, philosophy, ethnicity, gender, background or choice of life style as long as each respects the freedoms and rights of all others.

Redundant world presidents and residences would allow cooperative sharing of decision making powers so that the likelihood that a sensible majority representing the will of most citizens throughout the global economy is adequately taken into consideration.

With a SECO government and a SANE economy linked together with the ShareFlow ECU network in operation, money would no longer be the fly in the ointment that traditionally holds back progress that could exponentially benefit all citizens including even the so-called wealthy elite.

It would be a grand awakening and a bold statement to all that these are the necessary ideas for the time that has finally arrived upon the scene of every human endeavor.

~31~
A Universal Metric System

To convert from a well established system of measure in anyone's imagination would be a hard sell indeed, and in fact could be the understatement of the century because it shouts out the popular cliché: 'If it isn't broke, don't fix it!'.

That is normally a truism, but in this case, it seems the case for 'unbroken' could be grossly underestimated.

To their credit, converting from the English measuring system to Base 10 metric has succeeded in many countries throughout the world, however nowhere has there been a greater resistance to making the change than in the halls of Congress of the United States Government over the years.

The reasons for resistance are based upon lack of public support because of generally accepted beliefs such as:

1. 'The system we use works well so why change?'
2. 'Change would be inconvenient to businesses.'
3. 'The costs would be prohibitive.'

Result: A sensible change for improving efficiency over an existing system such as this can never happen as long as there is the lack of vision by those in authority that claim future benefits are not worth the time and energy and…yes, too costly as the default excuse for conservative thinking.

However, when a sensible world government and a new economy based upon earned credit units are used in lieu of money comes along; traditional excuses for inaction may no longer apply for denying an idea whose time has come.

Indeed , it seems logical that when cost accountability is no longer a trump card in a game of action vs. suppression, the idea of converting to a universal metric system would seem much more than just a clever idea to be brushed aside in favor of 'more pressing issues at the moment'

When cost accountability is no longer a factor, it would seem that progressive thinkers could present a strong case that converting to a universal metric system of measure would allow for unrestricted efficiency to benefit science as well as the socioeconomics of business.

Unfortunately it's the sensible efficiency suggestions that our money-driven government cannot bring up for serious discussion to implement doable system changes.

If we can sell the idea that converting to a Universal System of Measure for the entire global community using the universally accepted Base 10 numbering system is a good idea, then talking about going to Base 10 metric makes good sense as a starting point for an even more ambitious venture in a moneyfree credit unit environment.

And the more ambitious idea is posed with a question -

What is there to prevent a well conceived plan for using an alternative numbering base; in fact what is there to stop us from taking the metric idea one step further (a giant step further) and consider implementing a global Base 16 metric system instead of a global Base 10 metric conversion?

Is that too radical? - I don't think so.

For one thing, a Base 16 system would be more efficient and more compatible to the way computers and computer hardware functions are set up for efficiency to operate, since Base 16 uses multiples of 2 for the manipulation of bits and bytes of information in all computations.

Data storage has been historically accomplished in word sizes of 8, 16, 32 or 64 bit lengths for ease and speed of data manipulation, and provides greater speed and efficiency in accessing and storing information for elaborate displays and for subsequent calculations.

That is why I would make the rather audacious claim (at least to the politicians and pragmatists) that converting to Base 16 would be even more advantageous and not that much more trouble than the easier route but less interesting practicality of conversion to universal Base 10 metric that we are already familiar with.

Now before getting too pragmatic by saying that Base 10 works well so why fix it?, how about considering Base 16 numbering in light of the advantages that would be present when using it for all measurements as a universal metric?

By doing so, we could create a system to factor most every variable with convenient powers of 2 for mathematical precision in scientific formulation over the entire range of scientific and practical quantifications and retain the ease of using factors of 2 for many mathematical operations we may find a bit complex in calculations for clear understanding.

Let's take a look at what a Base 16 metric system would look like compared to what we already use as Base 10.

With 10 unique single digits to represent the alphabet of numbering in either the English or the Metric standard of quantification, we still have the complexities of requiring many non-integral conversion factors for measurement of units needed when going from one system to the other.

Commonly referred to as the hexadecimal system, Base 16 defines the first tier of single digit representation as going from 0-15 instead of 0-9, with the designation 10 beginning the tier of 2-digit numbers for hexadecimal instead of 10 beginning the 2-digit numbers in the decimal system.

For larger numbers, equivalences are written as follows:
10 (hexadecimal) = 16 (decimal)
100 (hexadecimal) = 256 (decimal)
1000 (hexadecimal) = 4096 (decimal)
10000 (hexadecimal) = 65536 (decimal), etc.

For numbers proceeding in the other direction of measure known as fractions we have examples as follows:
1/10 (hexadecimal) = 1/16 (decimal)
1/100 (hexadecimal) = 1/256 (decimal)
1/1000 (hexadecimal) = 1/4096 (decimal)
1/10000 (hexadecimal) = 1/65536 (decimal), etc.

31 A Universal Metric System

Similarly for designating powers as decimal places of the base number we get the following simple examples:

$0.1 = 10^{-1}$ (hexadecimal) $= 0.0625$ (decimal)

$0.01 = 10^{-2}$ (hexadecimal) $= 0.00390625$ (decimal)

$0.001 = 10^{-3}$ (hexadecimal) $= 0.00024414$ (decimal)

$0.0001 = 10^{-4}$ (hexadecimal) $= 0.000015258$ (decimal)

As science advances, the need for expressing numbers easily will become more important in the evolving increase of extent needed in the macro (ultra-large) and the micro (ultra-small) direction.

In this instance, logic says that striving for conciseness is one good reason for using Base 16 exclusively; and once it became more familiar to the general population for everyday use, the ease and efficiency for use in all levels of human development such as science, education, engineering and even the business world should become more apparent.

With adequate public education it would logically speak volumes about some necessary changes in the way we think about numbers, mathematics and virtually every field of science and the medical profession of complex formulas.

There are good reasons why the hexadecimal standard could be defended as the only sensible standard worth the time and money to convert to instead of Base 10 Metric.

To start, we could say that converting to Base 16 Metric might help the general populace learn greater appreciation for science, and the use of a beautifully new and efficient way of expressing mathematical operations.

This might be emphasized even more considering some of the cumbersome uses of English as the standard; but let's just consider a few advantages that become more defensible when money is no longer a wall of suppression.

In order to extend our universal Base 16 metric system to the definitions used in science that make computations easier to deal with, I am suggesting that we begin with a unit of time defined and considered as the fundamental Unit of Scientific Measure arbitrarily referred to as a **Vib.**

For our example, the **Vib** might be defined arbitrarily as (16^{16}) atomic frequency vibrations of the oxygen atom.

For illustration purposes, let us assume that this small fraction of time came to approximately 0.65018 traditional Earth seconds, and that the name of this fundamental unit of measure is referred to as the **Vib.**

With this unit defined as the base unit of time, all other units of measure could theoretically be derived to keep every unit free of the need to convert to any alternate system of measure, such as English, Base 10 Metric or complex units within Base 16 itself.

Using mathematical equivalency and suitable powers of 16 (or convenient powers of 2), we can derive three more fundamental units to define the Base Units of Measure (one each for time, space, energy and mass).

This logic lends itself to form the basis for derivation of other convenience units in the Universal Metric System of Measure using Base 16 with the four Base Units as the basis for equivalency equations as follows:

With C being the speed of light, E being energy and M representing mass, we have Einstein's equation stated as:

Energy = Mass x (Speed of Light) ^{2} =M x C^2 getting

C = the square root of (E/M), and since Distance =

Space = Rate x Time, we get a single relationship involving all the basic quantifications in the physical universe using equivalency relationships with the ultimate rate C:

C = Space/Time = the Square Root of (Energy/Mass).

Using these equations, we can define the relationships of the Base Units conveniently as follows.

The Base Unit of Time:

T = 16^{16} Vibs = 1 UMS Second.

The Base Unit of Space:

S = C x T = 1 UMS Meter.

The Basic Unit of Mass:

M = the mass of one photon =1 UMS Spec

with a 1 UMS Meter wavelength

31 A Universal Metric System

The Base Unit of Energy:

E = the energy of 16^{16}photons = 1 UMS Erg.

Other units called Standard Units can be calculated for convenience in measuring other quantifications observed and derived in nature and can ultimately be derived with mathematical formulas involving the Base 16 Units.

Reiterating the rationale for considering the hexadecimal system as the one a global network economy should use for a standard, we know that all computers use hexadecimal for word storage and computation.

And we know that the Base 16 metric idea becomes a natural way to think about numbers for other reasons as well since it lends itself to observed processes in nature with the related use of other powers of 2 where necessary.

With a system of natural numbers like hexadecimal, we can go so far as to create Universal Metric Time by replacing the common units of time we now adhere to with a sensible system of hexadecimal and related powers of 2.

Metric time would not need to be synchronized with the Earth's revolution around the sun; however for another reason I suggest that we might constrain the Base 16 metric day to be synchronous with the Earth's period of rotation.

With Base 16 metric as the new standard referred to as the Universal Metric System, simple multiples of 2 are much more convenient and natural to use than trying to adhere to an exclusive use of powers of 16 alone.

I would like to suggest a rationale for considering the hexadecimal Base 16 number system to replace Base 10 as the standard for a global network economy that would use a unified system of quantification set up specifically for deriving convenience units of time.

Base 16 lends itself quite naturally to processes and structuring observed in nature with the use of alternate powers of 2 as part of the rationale.

With a system of natural numbers like Base 16 that can adapt to using alternate powers of 2 when necessary, we

261

can create a logically planned universal metric time system by replacing the measurements of time we now use with a new method using Base 16 Metric exclusively.

By doing so, the entire global community could learn an exciting, interesting and practical way of thinking about time as well as numbers in general with only powers of 2 needed for easy factoring to describe other units.

As examples of time divisions for everyday use that might closely resemble the units we are all familiar with, I am suggesting the following table of equivalences that the UMS system of time could use.

But first let's adjust the UMS second to be equal to approx.0.6501796875 standard seconds (about 2/3 the value of a standard second) in order to have the UMS Day stay synchronized with the Earth's rotation:

With that baseline we get the following values:

64 UMS Seconds = 1 UMS Minute
64 UMS Minutes = 1 UMS Hour
32 UMS Hours = 1 UMS Day (24 standard hours)
8 UMS Days = 1 UMS Week
32 UMS Days = 4 UMS Weeks = 1 UMS Month
8 UMS Months = 256 UMS Days = 1 UMS Year

This is only one suggestion out of many possibilities; however it can make a lot of sense while upholding our sense of having a day equal to what we are accustomed to.

This plan would rigorously adhere to the exclusive use of powers of 2 and would use an equivalence adjustment of one UMS second to synchronize to Earth's rotation.

In so doing, it would be asynchronous in terms of days in the UMS Year compared to the traditional year having 365.25 days that we are all accustomed to.

But since there are already some arguably illogical and bizarre divisions in the system we use now, for example: (February 28 days, leap year with 29, and 30 or 31 days in the other months, 7 days a week, 365.25 days in a year, irregular time zones, daylight savings time, etc. many of us are willing to conclude that the new system would be a good thing once adjusted to for everyday use.

Logically it would be a good thing to replace all of the irregularities with a UMS hexadecimal number system that relies only on factoring with powers of 2 throughout.

What about New Year's Day? - No problem!

Beginning day of the Seasons? - No problem!

Traditional Holidays? - Again - No problem!

All the special days of the year can be noted in terms of posting calendar dates that vary but can become more commonplace once familiarity sets in.

By having well-planned educational material to present to the population explaining all the reasons why Base 16 Metric makes good sense, each of us would do well to take a simple but interesting online course to get accustomed to what to expect when changes are finally implemented.

Logical as it may sound to many, I see that it could not gain sufficient support for implementation until money is replaced with a new global economy using earned credit units to take away the 'no can do' attitude that so many of us have ingrained in our usual pragmatic way of thinking.

~32~
The Self-Construct Mechanism

Is it not an insidious form of ignorance that allows the money-driven world of business and government to forge our destiny and limit our reasoning to recognize the real values that make life worth living?

Are not misplaced values based upon out-of-control monetary accountability the true basis of suppression that ignores necessary change and contributes to the decline in quality of life for so many?

Is the culture of competition that forces money to act as the only necessity in life for the masses a real cause and effect of a self-destruct mechanism that threatens our very existence as a human social structure?

Think about it...

America has enjoyed what many consider a profoundly high standard of living compared to many other countries throughout the rest of the world.

Still it never gets on track to use its full potential to create the meaningful improvements that even the upper class would recognize as necessary and achievable.

The old cliché: 'The rich get richer and the poor get poorer' has said it all since time immemorial as it still does today with respect to society's basic enigma of ignoring a vast segment of the world's population in favor of a cruel mindset that allows the gap between the wealthy and the poor to expand indefinitely.

Since there are no effective laws in place to stop them, the so-called wealthy 'elite' hoard most of the money by effectively taking it out of circulation and end up using it for power and control of the less fortunate who are usually helpless to change the dynamics.

Incredibly, the leaders of nations have never been able to truly grasp the real truth of how this endless drama has affected the lives and well-being of everyone on the planet in so many ways.

But the real kicker to this self-limiting way of living is the fact that the inevitable consequences of living this way ends up substantially hurting the lives of even the wealthy themselves in so many ways they can't imagine.

For generations, the money controlling conservatives in government have preached a smoke screen of cover up and distractions regarding the important issues, and have been unstoppable with their prattle over 'crushing national debt' and 'runaway' government spending'.

Of course, ignorance of the real problems and timidity among liberals and 'center of the road' thinkers have not allowed any serious challenges to this irrational arrogance, control and domination.

The more rational thinkers understand that debt and runaway spending are not the most important concerns.

In recent years it has become abundantly clear to them that virtually all symptoms of economic distress boil down to problems with the system itself.

Simply put, money itself has not been allowed to get to where it really needs to go so it can do the most good for the economy and the citizens who support it.

Many who call themselves progressive have historically realized that money is supposed to be only a tool for the convenient exchange of products and services based upon the philosophy of value given for value received.

From a rational thinking perspective, money was never meant to be a mechanism to assert power to control and maintain unethical advantage over others.

The underlying philosophy of 'value given for value received' is very simple in theory but has not been applied in a way that would be fair and equitable for everyone in terms of disallowing unethical acquisition.

And this underscores the basic fault of the monetary system which inherently allows transfers of uncontrolled sums of money from one individual to another such that ethical use of money is no longer a strict requirement for many financial transactions.

The hoarding of funds in personal and business bank accounts give account holders the power to collectively use their extra money in fraudulent and unethical ways to often cause severe imbalance to the economy and resultant financial disaster to those forced to struggle for the basics.

Progressives see the higher truth about the way we are supposed to use money, and they recognize that money is supposed to be a convenient means to the end goal of providing a steadily improving quality of life for everyone.

To achieve a truly healthy and adequate flow of money within an economy, the potential energy of many citizens working together is necessary for the motivation of change and a means to bring true economic benefit to all.

In this day and age, most economic systems seem to operate quite differently, with no one in charge to see that balance is maintained with unfettered opportunities for everyone to reach their full potential regardless of their status of who they are or where they live.

Capitalism is quite notorious for operating in a mode of competiveness since it is never well planned but simply allowed to shift and drift along with the laws of supply and demand regardless of existing logic that could make it work better for every citizen at any level.

Socialistic economies are better at seeing that a balance is maintained to avoid a gap between the wealthy and the poor; however they fail at expanding the potential that a logical system of self-construct dynamics could do to bring abundance and peaceful living to everyone on the planet.

32 The Self-Construct Mechanism

As I and many other progressives see it, a philosophy of holding religiously (literal meaning intended) to a strict standard of economic conservatism inevitably results in a system that is not anywhere near our true potential.

It is becoming more apparent that the philosophy of cutting government spending based upon obsession and loyalty to religious ideologies tends to force economic stagnation and inefficiency at best and threatens the downfall of civilization at its worst.

Instead, the true value of free-flowing money in the economy can best be measured by steady changes that can take place over time and specifically upon how standards of living and quality of life can improve for the average citizen as a result of those changes.

When there is real evidence that an efficient system is put into place to deliver benefits and improvements for every citizen in a self-sustaining manner, the maintenance of these policies is what I call a self-construct mechanism.

By definition, the self-construct mechanism I have in mind would be recognized as a system that could reliably discourage the goal of pursuing money, power and control in favor of encouraging the alternate reality that allows a natural way to embrace higher values and the qualities of living that are independent of monetary concerns.

It would be a major shift in thinking outside the box that we all need in order to lead every citizen along the path to a sensible economy, a high standard of living and a pollution-free environment for everyone.

It would be a mechanism to maintain fair exchange for all available abundance to flourish without threat or harm from anyone who might still live in pursuit of wealth to maintain power and control of the disadvantaged.

Logically I know of no one who would not agree that in theory, a self-construct mechanism would be a good thing, and would be preferable to the alternatives of financially-

267

driven destruct monopolies that allow money to become the God-like entity that defines the prime objective and the number one priority of human existence.

Establishing a moneyfree world based upon the philosophy of value given for value received using only non-transferable earned credit units in lieu of money is sensible logic and a sound basis for creating and maintaining the dynamics needed for a self-improving system that works for everyone.

Until money accountability as we know it is removed from the equation and mechanics of life, we cannot free ourselves of the burden of self-limitation not only in the physics of obtaining necessary goods and services, but also in the incentive to think outside the box for a whole lot of things so that the whole idea of self-improvement takes on a reality that naysayers and deniers can no longer derail.

The removal of money and money accountability will not only signal the death of money as we know it, but will also trigger the birth of a new civilization based upon the means of self-improvement in all facets of living.

These facets include world government, the economy, the arts and sciences, the healthcare industry, exclusive use of renewable clean energy and the support of education at all levels so that the entire global extent of socioeconomics is put into balance to help optimize the physical, mental, emotional and spiritual health of every citizen.

The concepts supporting a moneyfree economy and its inherent self-construct way of living need to be spread far and wide to the citizens of all nations.

And the practical means of implementation to that end need to become grounded into the psyche of our leaders to work together to accomplish that goal.

Attaining that priority goal will require an out-of-the-box effort by many throughout the world community to come together to collaborate for setting up a well-planned system that allows all products and services to be freely and fairly distributed to everyone without the unnecessary conscious thought of money being involved.

A system using earned credit units with a SECO based government, a SANE economy and the ShareFlow ECU network resulting from a step by step transition in the way we use money would be the logical means to develop all the resources needed for the creation of a new dynamic called the Self-Construct Mechanism that would work for everyone and not just the wealthy elite.

Educating the leaders and citizens of all nations to this end would result in unlimited opportunities for abundance that would be sustained by simple commitment to mutual trust and cooperation between all humans on the place we call Earth, and the location we chose for advancement in the process of educating ourselves and furthering our way along the eternal evolutionary path.

~

Conclusion

What has been presented in this story is only a guideline to what I see as logical for defining a sensible methodology for creating a global economy that works well for everyone.

For untold generations, the ultra-wealthy have believed that money gets them everything they need in life as they remain oblivious to their true potential for experiencing the real purpose of why they are living on this planet.

Money used for power makes it impossible for anyone in any government to support a plan for enacting a system that could make monumental improvements in the quality of life for every citizen including the ultra-wealthy.

Instead of power to control others, our leaders need to learn that mutual cooperation and trust to support human rights, liberties and ever-improving living standards can be achieved and maintained for every citizen and should be considered normal and not the unattainable.

Since it is apparent that money manipulation buys the elections of many unethical leaders having no thought of making things better for the working classes, we need to see a solution to the problem from a different perspective.

The real impetus however will have to come from many who must come together in a spirit of cooperation to define a goal that can take the whole concept seriously enough to offer support for educating the masses.

In this presentation I have outlined several ideas that I think can make a significant impact towards the goal of a virtually moneyfree world in as short a time as possible.

Borrowing the adage that says it's best to fight fire with fire, perhaps the analogy for our purpose here would be to consider fighting money with money.

Let us assume there are a few ethical billionaires who are smart enough to know that their status and money can be used to benefit society while getting significant payback as they put together a well-thought out plan to help others.

Their plan would create a sensible curriculum of public education using the media, our existing educational facilities and the entertainment industry to extol the concept of living in a moneyfree world too advantageous to ignore.

Advertising the advantages of the moneyfree idea in an entertaining way could result in a tsunami of interest and might even get an unstoppable ball rolling towards national attention and eventually significant global support.

Advertising moneyfree using these methods would be an obvious way of generating interest, along with various means of sparking interest in the world of sports, the music industry and pop cultural events with a gradually increasing focus on how 'moneyfree' works to everyone's advantage.

Using public and private educational material to present the moneyfree idea could be a challenging subject of general interest in the wider field of social studies curriculum.

As always, the content could be put into the appropriate format for various age groups of children and youth as they attend classes throughout their general education years.

Here's a final thought and perhaps a significant irritation and annoyance to those who need to be annoyed...

What if our nation could have a well-financed lobbying effort to convince Congress to create an amendment to the U.S. Constitution that defines the sensible change of using earned credit units instead of traditional money in order to cyber-fund the entire global economy as the only logical end game for a global transition leading to a peaceful world?

What if...? Think about it!

271

A SHORT GLOSSARY OF TERMS

Cybermoney – Legal monetary value stored electronically by configuration of computer bits representing numbers.
Earned Credit Units – Wages paid in cybermoney that cannot be transferred to anyone except the wage earner.
Economic Umbrella –Inclusion of specific products and services that are paid for by contributions from everyone in the general population.
ECU Network – Earned Credit Unit Network that deals with credit units for wage dispensations and purchases.
Invisible Tax – Tax money that is paid in lieu of all other taxation and already included in the price of purchases.
Infinite Ocean – The unlimited source of credit units in the ECU Network that is available for all transactions.
Moneyfree – A relative term to illustrate various levels of independence from monetary concerns including the entire removal of money from our system.
Moneyclot – The obstruction of a free flow of money in the economy due to malevolent hoarding by the wealthy.
Monetary Accountability – The various requirements of accountability that are imposed on everyone to see that bills and taxes are paid regardless of one's ability to pay.
One World Government – A governing authority set up to have jurisdiction over all nations globally.
SCM – Self Construct Mechanism – A cooperative way of living that has the means to self-improve over time.
Self-Construct Co-Operacy – A world government that operates on the principles of mutual trust and cooperation among all its citizens.
ShareFlow – The world banking system that uses only a standard of global cybermoney of earned credit units.
Sharo – A unit of currency in terms of universal money prior to the global transformation into earned credit units.
UIP – The Universal Insurance Program defined as a subdivision of the SANE economic model of operation.

SANE Economy – The Socially Automated Network Economy – as described with seven subdivisions that would work together for the benefit of all citizens.

Social Umbrella – The Economic Umbrella that operates in a socialistic form of government.

Universal Metric System –A proposed alternative to the Base 10 Metric System using Base 16 numbering that could work well under a united world government.

Universal Language – A proposed language designed from scratch to be efficient in the five aspects of reading, writing, speaking, listening and computer operations to replace the general use of all other languages globally.

Yuna – A unit of universal earned credit units proposed for use in place of money as we know it.

UMIP – The Universal Minimum Income Program as a subdivision of the SANE economic model of operation.

ABOUT THE AUTHOR

Alan Halverson is 80 years of age at the time of this publication. Alan's birth and early years were in Chicago, IL where he developed a compelling interest in astronomy, general science and mathematics.

Later he spent two years in the U.S. Army in Ohio and Maryland and completed his college education at Brigham Young University in Provo, Utah with a B.S. Degree in Physics and Mathematics.

His professional life included employment at a number of aerospace firms including NASA-Goddard Space Flight Center in Greenbelt, MD and Ball Research Corporation in Boulder CO as a computer programmer.

Alan's philosophy about life evolved away from early evangelical religious teachings through a number of other church affiliations including the Mormon philosophy.

His present belief system bypasses all of that in favor of a more personal attunement to the concepts of truth, light and love freely available to all regardless of affiliation.

A firm believer that we as humans on Earth are eternal souls having lived many lifetimes in various incarnations according to our own choice to gain experience and education, he knows that we can all reach higher levels of truth and love in order to share the joys of spiritual living with many others also seeking the greater truth.

Alan identifies as a messenger to the masses to help build a new world of trust and cooperation based upon justice, equality and freedom from the slavery of money and monetary accountability in favor of a new system.

From a unique but simple definition of moneyfree that Alan presents, he discusses a bold but simple philosophy regarding logical steps to achieve the end game of a global economy released from the limitations of a profit-driven mindset that is based upon endless money manipulation.

Recommended Reading

The End of Money: Toward a New World Economy
    Under the Credit Unit System
    By Darrel W. Kimble
        ISBN: 0972015108

The Moneyless Manifesto:
    Live Well, Live Rich, Live Free
    By Mark Boyle
        ISBN: 978-1-86253-101-5

The Seven Virtues of a Free and Equal Society:
    A Guide To Social Engineering
    By C.L. Stadler
        ISBN: 9781502961556

Sacred Economics:
    Money, Gift and Society in the Age of Transition
    By Charles Eisenstein
        ISBN: 978-1-58394-397-7

Blueprint for a Golden Society:
    By J.S. Boehme
        ISBN: 1475181892

The Game:
    Nothing is as it seems
    By Heather Macauley Noel and Kelly Cavanaugh
        ISBN-13: 978-1530275236

For Additional Copies of Moneyfree

Check for Title and Author for
Purchase on Amazon Books

For Additional Information visit:

http://www.starlightpoint.com/books

Or

Contact the Author by Email at:

hal2128ad@msn.com

The author encourages readers to
Take the opportunity to go to
www.amazon.com/books/moneyfree/
To give an honest customer review
Of what you have just read.
~
If desired, you may responsibly
Copy or quote material
For postings on
Facebook or
Twitter